THE WEST COAST LINES

BR STEAM
FROM EUSTON
TO GLASGOW

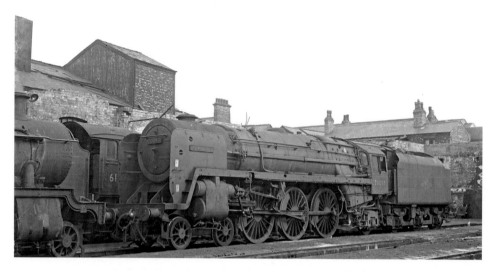

Crewe North 70053

Nos 70050-70054, the final five members of BR's Standard Class 7, were allocated to Polmadie Shed, Glasgow, when entering service and from there would have worked north-east to Perth and south to Carlisle. No. 70053 *Moray Firth* arrived at Polmadie ex-Crewe Works in September 1954. The last five engines have similar allocation histories and all had spells at Crewe North shed and later spent time at Banbury then Carlisle Kingmoor at the end of their careers. Crewe North became a major stabling point for the class during the first half of the 1960s (twenty-six by 1965), as they replaced withdrawn Royal Scots, Jubilees and Coronation Pacifics, mainly working north to Carlisle. The locomotive was scrapped after it left service in April 1967.

Carlisle Upperby Shed 45070

The first shed at Upperby was opened by the Lancaster & Carlisle Railway in 1846 to the south of Citadel station. The shed saw a number of cosmetic changes before it was completely remodelled by the LNWR in 1875, with the construction of a straight shed with eleven roads. No. 45070 emerged from Crewe Works in May 1935 with a 21 element superheater with 1¼ in. elements; it was only one of five built with this arrangement. It received a domed boiler in September 1958 and carried the type until its withdrawal in May 1967.

THE WEST COAST LINES

BR STEAM FROM EUSTON TO GLASGOW

FROM THE BILL REED COLLECTION

PETER TUFFREY

FONTHILL

Stirling Station 45423

At the south end of Stirling station on 7 April 1957 are two LMS Stanier Black Fives, nos 45400 and 45423. They are passing Stirling Middle signal box, which was one of three that marshalled the traffic in the station and immediate vicinity. It was opened on 4 August 1901 with ninety-six levers and refurbished in the 1950s, with the interior layout changed; the building is still extant. Both locomotives were built by Armstrong Whitworth & Co.; the dates were August and October 1937 respectively. No. 45400 was withdrawn in May 1964 whereas no. 45423 survived until May 1967.

Fonthill Media Limited
Fonthill Media LLC
www.fonthillmedia.com
office@fonthillmedia.com

Published in 2013

British Library Cataloguing in Publication Data:
A catalogue record for this book is available from the British Library

ISBN 978-1-78155-207-0

Typeset in 8.5pt on 11pt Sabon LT
Printed and bound in England

Connect with us
 facebook.com/fonthillmedia    twitter.com/fonthillmedia

Contents

Acknowledgements

I am grateful for help of the following people: Cathryn at Book Law (Nottingham), Hugh Parkin, Bill Reed, and Alan Sutton. Special thanks to my son Tristram Tuffrey for his general help behind the scenes. I have taken reasonable steps to verify the accuracy of the information in this book but it may contain errors or omissions. Any information that may be of assistance to rectify any problems will be gratefully received. Please contact me by email: petertuffrey@rocketmail.com, or in writing: Peter Tuffrey, 8 Wrightson Avenue, Warmsworth, Doncaster, South Yorkshire, DN4 9QL.

Polmadie Shed 46221
Driver McAlpine poses in front of LMS Coronation Pacific no. 46221 *Queen Elizabeth*. The locomotive entered traffic from Crewe in June 1937 and by the end of the year had completed almost 31,000 miles. It had fifty-seven days out of service in 1937 for repairs undertaken on shed at Camden and also because it was not required for duties. During the year this picture was taken – 1957 – the locomotive accumulated 45,103 miles and was out of service for 117 days for the above reasons. It was also on works for thirty-five days for light intermediate repairs. The locomotive was allocated to Polmadie from November 1939.

Introduction

There were many changes to British railways in the 1950s and 1960s. One massive change which concerns us here was the switch from steam to diesel traction. This also meant a massive upheaval in the infrastructure which kept steam locomotives on the rails. Bill Reed's photographs marvellously capture all of this. We see very grimy steam locomotives on turntables, trundling along branch lines, pausing in sleepy stations, waiting to be watered or coaled, and finally on the scrap lines. Looking back now, more locomotives and more pieces of this infrastructure should have been saved. But we all know the 1950s and '60s was not really a time for nostalgia and reflection, but one of moving forward and embracing the new.

Bill took the pictures when it was a privilege, not to mention a rarity, to have a decent camera. He also took them at a time when it was not frowned upon, like it is today, to be interested in railways, take pictures of locomotives and collect locomotive numbers. It was only natural for young lads to have a desire to look at the vast, almost human engines with awe, because maybe their dads, granddads or even great granddads had been part of building or working them. For decades the railways had touched the lives of many families across the entire country. It is also amazing now to look at some of Bill's pictures and realise that he was standing on railway track when he took them, unhindered by authority, yet always behaving responsibly. His closeness to his subjects is breathtaking at times, as many of the pictures in this book demonstrate.

The pictures in this book were chosen from the many hundreds of 35 mm colour slides and black and white negatives Bill took on and off the route stretching from Euston to Glasgow and Stirling. The Cheltenham, Chipping Norton and Worcester pictures are included in order to show how far at times Bill travelled off the route. All the pictures roughly cover a period from the 1950s to the late 1960s.

Bill was born in Nottingham in 1933. During his younger days, his mother frequently took him to visit her sister in Hucknall, Nottingham, travelling from Bullwell on the Sentinel Steam Railcars no. 5192 *Rising Sun* and no. 51908 *Expedition*. Yet, he has been told that even before then, his paternal grandfather took him to watch trains at Bulwell Common. His grandfather was a retired driver, formerly on the MS&LR at Northwich. He came to Annesley, near Nottingham, to work on the GCR when it opened. Bill's father was also interested in transport, having been apprenticed at Broughs, the Bulwell motorcycle builders; after the Second World War he worked at Wrigley's Wagon Repair Works in Nottingham. He also had an allotment, conveniently situated at the side of the Great Central Line, overlooking Bulwell Common Sidings. To Bill, it was a trainspotter's paradise, and he bought his first stock book, Ian Allen's *ABC of British Locomotives*, in 1943.

When Bill left school, he became a messenger lad at Nottingham Victoria station enquiry office. He spent his lunch hours on the station platforms, where he first met Freddie Guildford, a well-known local railway enthusiast. In time, Freddie encouraged Bill to take photographs, develop films and make contact prints.

In 1950 Bill obtained a job as an engine cleaner, the first step in the long slow haul to becoming a driver. The progress was interrupted by National Service, but he joined the RAF photographic club and was a member long enough to learn how to enlarge and print photographs.

Once demobbed, Bill bought an Agfa Super Isolette, which in 1955 was considered to be a very good camera. Bill returned to work at British Rail as a fireman on steam engines, including 4Fs, 8Fs and Class 5s. In 1966 he was passed for driving, but had to wait thirteen years before being made a regular driver. Unfortunately, by that time, steam had long since given way to diesel.

Throughout his life, Bill has always taken black and white photographs, colour slides and cine film of railways in this country, Eastern and Western Europe, and America. Bill used a Mamiya 330 for most of his black and white photography, but he also used 35 mm Practicas, a Canon for colour, and a Bolex 8 mm cine.

Many of the pictures reproduced here were taken by Bill after work at weekends or during annual holidays. Frequently using his rail passes, taking advantage of organised 'railway trips', or riding as a passenger on a friend's motorbike, he would find interesting locations where steam locomotives were still operating.

Many of the well-known sheds where vast numbers of locomotives were allocated were a source of much inspiration for Bill. For example, he was very active shooting film at Camden, Willesden, Derby, Crewe, Carlisle and Glasgow Polmadie, and at times it was very difficult to know what to include and what to leave out of this book.

I have noted in the text the history of many of these sheds and, where appropriate, their status today. I also present extensive histories of the locomotives, including where they were built, where they were allocated, work schedules and, if known, their final destiny.

But what is remarkable about this book is the vast number of locomotive classes included in both the British and Scottish sections. The task of documenting them was enormous as the long bibliography at the back testifies.

The new 'green' diesels shown here look remarkably modern and more efficient than their steam counterparts, and that is why they have been included – as a stark contrast to their predecessors. But many of them have, in turn, given way to electrics in the intervening years.

Looking back now at the 1950s and 1960s, Bill says he would have taken many more pictures of steam locomotives. But that is no matter; he has taken more than enough to give us a good idea of what it was like in those last days.

CHAPTER 1

London Euston to Rugby Shed

London Euston 46170

Taken at London Euston station, the photograph features LMS Fowler 'Royal Scot' Class 4-6-0 no. 46170 *British Legion*, which was built by the North British Locomotive Company in December 1929. The station was opened by the London & Birmingham Railway on 20 July 1837 to the design of Philip Hardwick, and constructed by William Cubitt. The first services ran to present-day Hemel Hempstead and it was not until September 1838 that a service to Birmingham was available. The building saw periodic expansion works from the late 1840s until the late 1890s. No. 46170 *British Legion* was withdrawn from Llandudno Junction in December 1962.

London Euston 46138

Another Royal Scot has been pictured at Euston station, this time it is no. 46138 *The London Irish Rifleman*, which has paused at Platform 1. The original station was demolished in the early 1960s and replaced by a building designed by British Rail and Richard Seifert & Partners and built by Taylor Woodrow Construction Ltd. The number of platforms was increased from fifteen in the original station to eighteen in the new. At the time of the picture the locomotive was allocated to Crewe North shed where it had a number of spells during the 1950s. Its last shed was Carlisle Upperby and it left service from there in February 1963.

Camden 45526

This LMS Fowler 5XP, later 6P, 'Patriot' Class 4-6-0 locomotive no. 45526 *Morecambe and Heysham* is seen here at Camden shed in 1951. It is still to receive smoke deflectors and have the BR emblem applied to the tender. No. 45526 was built at Derby Works in March 1933 but was not named until October 1937. It then took the name of the two resorts served by the London, Midland & Scottish Railway. The locomotive was based at Carlisle Upperby shed at the time of the photograph, arriving there in September 1950 having previously been allocated to Edge Hill shed. It spent the rest of its career operating from Carlisle and was withdrawn from the shed in October 1964.

Camden 46125

LMS Fowler 6P, BR classification 7P from 1951, Royal Scot locomotive no. 46125 *3rd Carabinier* is pictured at Camden shed in 1951. The engine was among the first members of the class to emerge in 1927. Fifty were initially ordered from the North British Locomotive Company and construction was split between the firm's Queens Park and Hyde Park Works. As LMS no. 6125, the locomotive was the first of twenty-five to appear from Hyde Park Works between August and November. The engine was originally to be named *Lancashire Witch* after the one built by Robert Stephenson & Co. in 1828, but it was renamed to fall into line with other members of the class which were named after army regiments. No. 46125 was withdrawn from Annesley in October 1964.

Camden 46245

This image of LMS Stanier 'Coronation' Pacific no. 46245 *City of London* was taken at Camden shed on 31 March 1963. The locomotive was built at Crewe Works towards the end of June 1943, fully streamlined, and was the first new member of the class to appear since 1940. Three other Coronation engines were built in 1943, and out of the four, only one, LMS no. 6246 *City of Manchester*, was built with a new boiler, the others receiving reconditioned LMS type 1X boilers. *City of London* was a long-term resident at Camden shed, and when this picture was taken, it was only a few months away from moving to Willesden in September. The locomotive was moved again in July 1964 to Crewe North, but was withdrawn in October and scrapped by the end of the year at Cashmore's Great Bridge scrapyard.

Camden 46155

Derby Works constructed a further twenty members of the Royal Scot class between May and November 1930, with no. 46155 *The Lancer* entering service in July. Of these locomotives, the final fourteen were built with new piston valve seals as the original type was causing large leakages of steam when wear occurred. The other members of the class were also subsequently altered. In the BR period the locomotive saw a number of transfers between sheds, with its main residence being Crewe North, but punctuated with stays at Camden, Holyhead and Edge Hill. At the time of the photograph, 31 March 1963, no. 46155 was allocated to Llandudno Junction and would return to Crewe North at the end of June. *The Lancer*'s final allocation was to Carlisle Kingmoor and was withdrawn from the shed in December 1964.

Camden 46245

Another view of Coronation Pacific no. 46245 *City of London* at Camden shed, but this time from the front end. The first engine shed at Camden was built by the London & Birmingham Railway and opened in June 1837 at the east end of Chalk Farm station. This was then replaced by a roundhouse in 1847, which was in use until the early 1870s. It was then used as a store before becoming The Roundhouse arts centre. Also, in 1847 a straight shed was built south of the roundhouse for passenger engines, with five tracks and open at either end. The shed was modified by the LMS in 1932 with the addition of a further two tracks and a larger turntable. The mechanical coal stage seen behind *City of London* was installed in the early 1920s by the London & North Western Railway. Steam locomotives left the shed in September 1963 and it was closed completely at the beginning of 1966.

Harrow and Wealdstone Station 45740

LMS Stanier 5XP, later 6P, 'Jubilee' Class 4-6-0 locomotive no. 45740 *Munster* is seen hauling an express freight train on the up fast line at Harrow and Wealdstone station. Built at Crewe Works in December 1936, the locomotive was the third to last engine of the class to be built. Construction of the Jubilees had started in 1934 and took place at Derby, Crewe and the North British Locomotive Co. Members of the class eventually totalled 191, with the numbers produced at each works being 10, 131 and 50 respectively. No. 45740 left service in October 1963.

Harrow and Wealdstone Station 45740

Another view of no. 45740 *Munster* passing through Harrow and Wealdstone station. The station was built by the London & Birmingham Railway in July 1837 and was known as Harrow station until Wealdstone was added to the name in May 1897. At this time it was operated by the London & North Western Railway. The station was the scene of a serious crash in October 1952 involving three trains, which killed 112 and injured 340. The section of footbridge seen to the right of the locomotive was destroyed during the crash and was subsequently rebuilt. A Jubilee Class locomotive was destroyed, no. 45637 *Windward Islands*, along with Princess Royal Class no. 46202 *Princess Anne*. Coronation Class no. 46242 *City of Glasgow* was also badly damaged but was repaired and re-entered service.

Harrow and Wealdstone Station 48615

LMS Stanier 8F Class 2-8-0 locomotive no. 48615 is running light on the up fast line at Harrow and Wealdstone station. The LMS constructed 331 8F locomotives between 1936 and 1945. The War Department built 208 examples and a further 313 members of the class were built under order from the Railway Executive Committee during the Second World War. Many different works were involved in the construction of 8Fs during the War including: NBLC, Beyer, Peacock and Co. (both for WD), Swindon, Darlington, Doncaster, Eastleigh and Ashford (REC). Locomotive no. 48615 was built at Brighton Works in September 1943 as part of an order from the REC for sixty-eight 8Fs. A total of ninety-three were built at the works during the War; twenty-five of these were loaned to the LNER and classified O6 by them, but they were returned to the LMS at the end of the conflict. Some 666 worked on British rails after the War, and no. 48615 was in service until February 1966.

Willesden 46240

LMS Coronation Pacific no. 46240 *City of Coventry* was allocated to Willesden shed between September 1963 and August 1964, and the picture probably dates from this time. The locomotive had spent the preceding twenty-three years as a resident at Camden shed, and prior to that, a month at Crewe North shed, having been built at the town's works in March 1940. *City of Coventry* is seen in LMS lined maroon livery, which had been applied in August 1960. The locomotive had also carried the BR lined maroon, BR green, BR blue, LMS lined black, plain black and was originally LMS maroon. *City of Coventry* was one of three engines to carry the armorial crest of the city it was named after, while no. 46220 *Coronation* carried a crown above its name. No. 46240 was withdrawn in October 1964 and subsequently scrapped.

Willesden 70054

British Railways Standard Class 7 'Britannia' Pacific no. 70054 *Dornoch Firth* was the last of the class to be built. Emerging from Crewe Works in September 1954, it was allocated to Polmadie shed. Upon entering service the locomotive was not named, but *Dornoch Firth* had been acquired by February 1955. The locomotive is showing the Willesden shed code on the smokebox door despite being officially allocated to Crewe North at the time of the picture. No. 70054 was withdrawn at the end of November 1966 with a disappointing service life of just over twelve years. The locomotive was scrapped by Motherwell Machinery & Scrap Co. in May 1967.

Willesden 78038

British Railways Standard Class Two 2-6-0 locomotive no. 78038 is pausing at Willesden shed to take on water. The locomotive was built at Darlington Works in November 1954 and went into service operating from Bescot on freight and local passenger services. No. 78038 had spells at Chester Northgate, Rhyl, and Northwich before arriving with a number of other Standard Class 2s at Willesden in May 1963. From the shed, their duties included: moving empty coaching stock, ballast trains, piloting, and occasional local passenger and freight services. No. 78038 was also used in 1964 for the Locomotive Club of Great Britain's 'Surrey Wanderer' Tour, along with Drummond M7 no. 30053. No. 78038 was in charge of the middle part of the trip between Shepperton and Caterham. The locomotive saw a final move to Shrewsbury in October 1965 and was withdrawn the following August.

Willesden 42730

LMS Hughes 'Crab' 2-6-0 locomotive no. 42730 was the first of the Crewe-built members of the class, entering service as LMS no. 13030 in November 1926. The works eventually produced 174 more examples of the design, constructing the last in December 1932. This was augmented by Horwich Works which made seventy 'Crabs' between June 1926 and December 1930. No. 42730 is seen at Willesden shed during the early 1960s with a tender still displaying LMS on its side, which would have been an unusual sight at the time. Withdrawal came in June 1965 from Stockport.

Willesden 70051

Willesden shed was built by the London & North Western Railway to the west of Willesden Junction station and on the south side of the lines. It opened in 1873 and was brick-built with twelve roads open at one end. The structure was enlarged by the company at the end of the nineteenth century with the addition of a similar building to the existing shed and with access extended to both ends. The LMS added a square roundhouse at the end of the 1920s, sited to the north-east of the earlier sheds. It closed to steam in August 1965 and became a Traction Maintenance Depot for electric locomotives. 'Britannia' Pacific locomotive no. 70051 *Firth of Forth* is pictured at the shed during the first half of the 1960s.

Ashchurch Station 47539

Leaving Ashchurch station with a passenger service bound for Upton-on-Severn is Fowler 0-6-0T Class 3, later 3F, locomotive no. 47539, built by William Beardmore & Co. in April 1928. The company produced ninety of the class between 1928 and 1929. Upton-on-Severn station closed to traffic on 14 August 1961. No. 47539 was withdrawn from service in February 1963 but was not scrapped by Cashmore's (Great Bridge) until January 1966.

Ashchurch Station 42417

Ashchurch station was opened by the Birmingham & Gloucester Railway in June 1840 and became part of the Midland Railway in 1846. The station was closed in November 1971 and the buildings were mostly cleared. However, the site was reopened for passengers on 30 May 1997, but the station was renamed Ashchurch for Tewkesbury. This picture shows Fowler Class 4P 2-6-4T locomotive no. 42417 leaving the station with a service bound for Birmingham via Evesham. This service ran on a loop line, also serving Alcester and Redditch, which was closed in June 1963, with the track south of Redditch removed. The tracks from Redditch to Birmingham, however, are still in use. No. 42417 was withdrawn in April 1964.

Bletchley 70032

Quick (2009) notes that Bletchley station was opened between 2 November 1838, when the preparations for the station are noted in company minutes, and 20 June 1839, its first appearance in the timetable. During the building's early existence it was also known as Bletchley and Fenny Stratford and Bletchley Junction for various periods, being exclusively Bletchley after 1870. Pictured at the station is BR Standard Class 7 locomotive no. 70032 *Tennyson*, built by Crewe Works in December 1952. It is a Willesden engine, displaying the 1A shed code, and it was resident there between January 1961 and October 1964. It was withdrawn from Carlisle Kingmoor shed in September 1967.

Leighton Buzzard 92020

British Rail Standard Class 9F 2-10-0 locomotive no. 92020 entered traffic from Crewe Works in March 1955. The engine was one of ten fitted with a Crosti boiler when built, which used exhaust gases to preheat the water used in the boiler. The system had found some success in Europe, but when used on the 9Fs, smoke was found to drift into the cab from the chimney on the side of the boiler and serious corrosion was also a problem. Modifications were made to the locomotives during the second half of the 1950s in an attempt to resolve these issues, however, it was eventually decided to fit conventional boilers. No. 92020 was in storage for almost two years between May 1959 and March 1961 awaiting attention; the conversion was finally completed in June 1961. The locomotive worked for a further six years before its withdrawal from Birkenhead in October 1967.

Leighton Buzzard 46209

LMS Stanier 'Princess Royal' Pacific locomotive no. 46209 *Princess Beatrice* is seen at Leighton Buzzard station. The engine was erected at Crewe Works in August 1935 as part of a second batch of ten locomotives. Two engines had been built previously at the works in 1933. Another member of the class was added in 1952 when the LMS 'Turbomotive' was rebuilt. The class was withdrawn in the early 1960s with no. 46209 leaving service from Camden shed in September 1962. Two of the class, no. 46201 *Princess Elizabeth* and no. 46203 *Princess Margaret Rose*, have been preserved.

Leighton Buzzard 48360

Two 8F 2-8-0s are pictured outside the shed at Leighton Buzzard. The first engine, no. 48360, has 50 per cent reciprocating balance and was built for the LMS at Horwich Works in July 1944. The number of the second engine is not identifiable. The shed at Leighton Buzzard was built by the LNWR in 1859 and was a simple facility with just two through roads. Few alterations were made to the building over the years with only a new roof being fitted in 1957. The shed closed five years later in November 1962 and has since been demolished. No. 48360 left service from Bletchley in July 1965.

Leighton Buzzard 84002

BR Standard Class 2 2-6-2T locomotive no. 84002 is pictured at Leighton Buzzard station with the passenger service to Dunstable. The station was opened in April 1838 by the London & Birmingham Railway but was later moved slightly to the south by the LNWR in 1859. It was called Leighton and Leighton Junction in the latter half of the nineteenth century and has been known as Leighton Buzzard since 1911. The branch line which this service operated on was laid by the LNWR and opened in 1848. It was a victim of the Beeching report and closed in 1965. The tracks have since been lifted.

Leighton Buzzard 84002

No. 84002 was erected at Crewe Works in August 1953 and was the third member of the class to be completed. Twenty were built at the works for local passenger services on the London Midland lines. A further ten were built at Darlington in 1957 and these went into service on the Southern Region lines. No. 84002's first allocation was to Bolton Plodder Lane shed before spells at Wrexham and Chester. It arrived at Bletchley in August 1956 and saw out its career working from the shed. Withdrawal came in April 1965.

Chipping Norton GWR 4100

The next few pictures show how, at times, Bill stepped off the West Coast route to take pictures elsewhere. Great Western Railway 5101 Class 2-6-2T locomotive no. 4100 is pictured at Chipping Norton station. The engine was built at Swindon Works and entered service in August 1935. A total of 140 engines of this class were completed to the design of Charles Collett, which was a progression of the GWR 3100 Class designed by George Churchward. No. 4100 is pulling the 16.53 Chipping Norton to Kingham passenger service. The first station serving the town was opened in August 1855 and built by the Chipping Norton Railway, connecting the town with the Oxford, Worcester and Wolverhampton Railway at Kingham. The CNR later became part of the Banbury & Cheltenham Direct Railway, which extended the line to King's Sutton; for this a new station was built at a new site, opening in April 1887. The line was leased by the GWR, who later took total control in 1897. Passenger services ceased in December 1962 and the line had been pulled up by 1965. No. 4100 was withdrawn in October of that year.

Cheltenham GWR 4101

GWR 5101 Class 2-6-2T locomotive no. 4101 entered traffic from Swindon Works in August 1935. It is photographed at Cheltenham Spa St James station with the 14.50 Cheltenham Spa St James to Kingham passenger service. The predecessor to this station was opened in October 1847 by the Cheltenham & Great Western Union Railway, which linked the town with Swindon. At this time the station was simply known as Cheltenham. The station was replaced by a new structure to the east of the original in September 1894. A further two name changes were implemented, the first from May 1908 when St James was added, then Spa from February 1925. Closure came in January 1966; the site was cleared and is now occupied by a supermarket. No. 4101 was withdrawn in June 1964 and scrapped; ten of the class have been preserved.

Worcester Shrub Hill GWR 5056

Worcester Shrub Hill station was opened on 5 October 1850 jointly by the Oxford, Worcester & Wolverhampton Railway and Midland Railway. Seen leaving the station in June 1963 is GWR Collett 4073 'Castle' Class 4-6-0 locomotive no. 5056 *Earl of Powis*, with the 15.10 to London Paddington station. The locomotive was built at Swindon Works in June 1936 and was originally named *Ogmore Castle*, the change occurring in September 1937. It was withdrawn from Oxley in November 1964 and scrapped at Cashmore's (Great Bridge) in February 1965. Eight of the 171 class members have been preserved.

Leamington Spa GWR 6029

GWR Collett 6000 'King' Class 4-6-0 locomotive no. 6029 *King Edward VIII* emerged from Swindon Works in August 1930 as *King Stephen*. It was renamed in May 1936 after the death of King George V. Construction of the class started in 1927 when twenty were produced, and these were followed by a further ten in 1930, no. 6029 being the last. The design was based on the 'Castle' Class, but the boiler was enlarged and so were the cylinders. No. 6209 is seen with the Cambrian Coast Express to London Paddington station. The service started in the summer of 1927 between London and Aberystwyth, with the London to Wolverhampton section of the journey being completed by a larger engine. The other half of the journey was headed by a smaller locomotive because of weight restrictions on the line. No. 6209 left service in July 1962 and had been scrapped by the end of the year at Cashmore's (Newport).

Rugby 92071

This photograph was taken on the 14 April 1962 from the Lower Hillmorton Road bridge at Rugby and is looking north, with Clifton Road bridge seen in the distance. The BR 9F locomotive is on the down line and is about to pass through Rugby Central station. The view from this site is completely different today as the tracks have been lifted, becoming a nature walk route. Also, the Lodge Plugs Ltd factory seen to the right on St Peter's Road has been demolished and replaced with new housing. No. 92071 was built at Crewe Works in 1956 then allocated to Doncaster shed. At the time of the picture the engine was based at Annesley, moving from Doncaster in March 1957. No. 92071 had a long allocation at the former, not moving again until July 1965 when it was transferred to Newton Heath. December 1965 saw the final move to Carlisle Kingmoor and the engine left service from the shed nearly two years later.

Rugby Central 44753

LMS Stanier 'Black Five' Class 4-6-0 locomotive no. 44753 is seen with a passenger service at Rugby Central station. The building was opened by the Great Central Railway in March 1899 when the line between Annesley and London Marylebone was completed. The station consisted of an island platform 600 ft long with waiting rooms and toilet facilities. The booking office was located on Hillmorton Road. No. 44753 emerged from Crewe Works in March 1948 with Caprotti valve gear and Timken roller bearings. The locomotive was a long-term resident at Leeds Holbeck shed, being allocated there from at least September 1950. In November 1963 it moved to Blackburn Lower Darwen shed and then at the end of the month to Southport. After a year working from Southport no. 44753 moved to Speke Junction until it was withdrawn in July 1965. Rugby Central was closed in May 1969 and the station buildings were removed, but the platform is still in existence.

Rugby Shed 58215

At Rugby shed is a Midland Railway Johnson 1357 Class 0-6-0 express goods, later LMS 2F Class engine no. 58215. It was built by Beyer, Peacock & Co. in January 1883 as one of eighty. No. 58215 was originally fitted with 17½ in. by 26 in. cylinders and a boiler with a pressure of 140 psi. Around 1916/17 an initiative was started to fit the locomotives with a Belpaire firebox. Also, the boiler pressure was increased to 160 psi and the cylinders were enlarged to 18 in. by 26 in. The locomotive had an impressive lifespan; it had been in service for just over seventy-eight years when withdrawal came when allocated to Rugby shed in March 1961.

Rugby Shed 40207

LMS Stanier 3P (BR 3MT) 2-6-2T locomotive no. 40207, built at Crewe Works in April 1938 as LMS no. 207, was one of the final members of the class to appear. The locomotive was erected with a LMS type 6A boiler with separate top-feed and dome. It was allocated at Warrington Dallam shed at Grouping but operated further south during the 1950s, with spells at Llandudno Junction, Bushbury Nuneaton and Willesden. Withdrawal from Nuneaton came in February 1962.

Rugby Shed 45599

While fifty-eight Jubilee Class locomotives were still to be built in the 1934 building programme at LMS-owned works, the company ordered a further fifty engines from the North British Locomotive Co., hoping they would be built and brought into service for the busy summer schedules. In the event the locomotives were delivered between June 1934 and February 1935. No. 45599 *Bechuanaland* was built by the NBLC's Queens Park Works and was delivered in January 1935. The NBLC engines were slightly different to others in the class as they were longer, had a different wheelbase, and were lighter. They were also fitted with a boiler made from nickel steel and a 4,000 gallon tender designed by Stanier. At the time of the photograph the locomotive was allocated to Willesden shed, and stayed there between November 1959 and January 1961. No. 45599 was withdrawn from Nuneaton shed in August 1964.

Rugby Shed 49441

This engine was completed for the LNWR at Crewe Works in September 1922 and was part of the G2 Class of 0-8-0 locomotives. They were designed by H. P. M. Beames while he was Chief Mechanical Engineer of the LNWR between 1920 and 1922. The locomotives were a development of the G1 Class and had a higher pressure boiler. The locomotive was allocated to Nuneaton when this photograph was taken. The allocation started in November 1958 after no. 49441 had arrived from Coventry shed and finished when it was withdrawn in October 1961.

Rugby 49342

A total of 170 LNWR Class B Four-Cylinder Compound 0-8-0 engines were produced to the design of Chief Mechanical Engineer Francis Webb. No. 49342 was erected at Crewe Works in October 1902. In the ensuing years the class was rebuilt into a number of different variations leaving only ten original locomotives to be withdrawn in the late 1920s. No. 49343 was rebuilt to Class G1 in December 1919, which meant it lost two cylinders and was superheated. The locomotive received a Belpaire firebox boiler in the late 1920s and was rebuilt again with a new boiler in October 1935 by the LMS. The locomotive was then classified G2A. No. 49342 completed its duties from Nuneaton until it was dispensed with in October 1961.

Rugby D219

English Electric Type 4, BR Class 40, diesel locomotive D219 *Caronia* entered traffic from Vulcan Foundry, Newton-le-Willows, in July 1959. It is pictured on the line close to Clifton Road and seen in the distance is Rugby Radio Station. This facility consisted of a very low frequency transmitter that came into use during January 1926 for broadcasting to the Commonwealth. In the 1950s the use was changed and messages were sent to submarines; the station was operational until the early 2000s. D219 was allocated to the London Midland Region when built and was among twenty-five chosen by that area to be named after ocean liners. *Caronia* was given to D219 in June 1962. The locomotive was withdrawn from service in December 1981 and was scrapped at Doncaster Works early in 1984.

Rugby 46244

With a passenger service, again near Clifton Road, is Coronation Pacific no. 46244 *King George VI*. Construction was completed in July 1940, and as no. 6244 it started its career from Camden shed. At this time the engine was called *City of Leeds*, following the naming of class members at the time; the change occurred in April 1941. 'City of Leeds' was later re-used on Coronation Pacific no. 46248. After a month on loan to Polmadie shed between September and October 1940, the locomotive returned to Camden shed, which was its base for the next eighteen years. Then came moves to Carlisle Upperby and Carlisle Kingmoor before withdrawal in October 1964. The task of scrapping the locomotive was carried out by Arnott Young.

Rugby 45631

Speeding past Clifton Road is Jubilee Class 4-6-0 locomotive no. 45631 *Tanganyika*. The engine was erected at Crewe Works in November 1934 with the LMS Crimson Lake livery with yellow and black lining applied. During the Second World War the locomotive was among a number of Jubilees that did not receive a plain black livery and remained in red throughout the duration of the conflict and its aftermath. The locomotive was repainted in August 1948 with the BR black livery with red, grey and cream lining. No. 45631 then had the BR Brunswick Green livery applied in September 1951; this scheme had become the standard for the class. Withdrawal from Crewe North came in August 1964.

Rugby D5074 and 44897

The old and the new meet close to Clifton Road at Rugby. The locomotives are: BR Class 24 no. D5074, built at Derby Works in March 1960, and LMS Stanier Black Five no. 44897, which emerged from Crewe Works in September 1945. The design for the Class 24 originated from Derby Works as part of the Pilot Scheme. Between 1958 and 1961, Derby, Crewe and Darlington produced 151 of the class. The locomotives were fitted with Sulzer 6LDA28 diesel engines and British Thomson-Houston generators. Originally, D5074 was allocated to March shed in the Eastern Region, but they were allegedly disliked by the crews there and were promptly displaced to other regions; D5074 found itself at Willesden then Watford. Withdrawal came in October 1975. No. 44897 saw the end of steam traction, leaving service in August 1968 from Carnforth shed.

Rugby 75052

The role of main designer for the BR Standard Class 4 4-6-0s was given to Brighton Works with Doncaster, Derby and Swindon playing a supporting role. The inspiration for the engines was drawn from LMS 2-6-4T locomotives, which in turn was the basis for the BR Standard Class 4 2-6-4T. Swindon Works was chosen to be the principle constructor of the class and eighty examples of the locomotives were produced there between 1951 and 1957. No. 75052 emerged in December 1956 and entered service to Bletchley shed. At the time of this photograph, taken from the area around Clifton Road at Rugby, no. 75052 was allocated to Willesden. It arrived there from Chester Northgate in January 1960 and left for Nuneaton in January 1963.

Rugby 46136

LMS Royal Scot 4-6-0 no. 46136 *The Border Regiment* is pictured at Rugby with an unidentified passenger service. Construction of the locomotive was carried out by the North British Locomotive Company's Hyde Park Works in September 1927, entering traffic as no. 6136 *Goliath*. The locomotive was rebuilt with new frames, cylinder and boiler in March 1950. All seventy Royal Scots underwent this transformation between 1943 and 1955. A further addition in the late 1950s or early 1960s was AWS, which is fitted to this locomotive as the protection place is seen below the bufferbeam. No. 46136 completed its time in service in March 1964.

Rugby 45523

LMS Fowler Patriot 4-6-0 locomotive no. 45523 *Bangor* emerged from Crewe Works in March 1933 and was withdrawn in January 1964 after a service life of close to thirty-one years. The locomotive had 3 ft 3 in. diameter leading wheels and 6 ft 9 in. diameter driving wheels. Engine and tender measured 62 ft 8¾ in. long. No. 45523 was allocated to Camden shed between July 1951 and January 1961 and then moved to Willesden. It was withdrawn from there in January 1964.

Rugby 44863

This image was taken on 14 October 1963 at the east end of Rugby Midland station (now just Rugby station) and shows Black Five no. 44863 leaving with an unidentified passenger service. The locomotive entered traffic from Crewe Works in January 1945 and had a career lasting twenty-two years, the end coming in May 1967. Rugby No. 1 signal box is seen behind the carriages and Rugby Power Signal Box behind the locomotive. Rugby No. 1 was built in 1884 by the LNWR with 180 levers (subsequently increased to 185). It closed in September 1964 when Rugby PSB started to handle the signalling of the station and the line as far as Castlethorpe. This box closed in May 2012 when its responsibilities were relinquished to Rugby Signalling Control Centre.

Rugby 46495

Seen from the same position as no. 44863, but to the right, is LMS Ivatt 2MT Class 2-6-0 locomotive no. 46495. Built at Darlington Works in January 1952, its first allocation was to Kettering. At the time of the photograph, the engine was allocated to 2B (Nuneaton), arriving there in May 1963. Behind the locomotive is Rugby shed's 300 ton capacity mechanical coaler, installed by the LMS as part of a modernisation scheme. No. 46495 was at Crewe North shed when it was condemned in October 1966.

Rugby 48012

Passing under the GCR bridge on the east side of Rugby Midland station is LMS Stanier 8F 2-8-0 locomotive no. 48012 constructed at Crewe Works in December 1936. During the Second World War the locomotive was one of fifty-one requisitioned by the War Department and took WD no. 577. It was put back into service for BR in December 1949 having been in store, and was then allocated to Rugby shed from February 1959, staying there until January 1965. Withdrawal from Edge Hill shed came in April 1968. The GCR bridge has since been demolished.

Rugby 49087

The LNWR G Class of 0-8-0s consisted of rebuilt and new engines to the design of George Whale. No. 49087 was a new engine and entered service from Crewe Works in February 1910; a total of sixty new engines entered traffic from the works during the year. The locomotive was rebuilt a number of times, its final incarnation being a G1 Class locomotive when it was overhauled by the LMS in June 1940. During the BR era, the engine was a long-term resident at Patricroft shed, from at least September 1950 until its withdrawal in September 1962. The engine is pictured at Rugby shed on 14 October 1963.

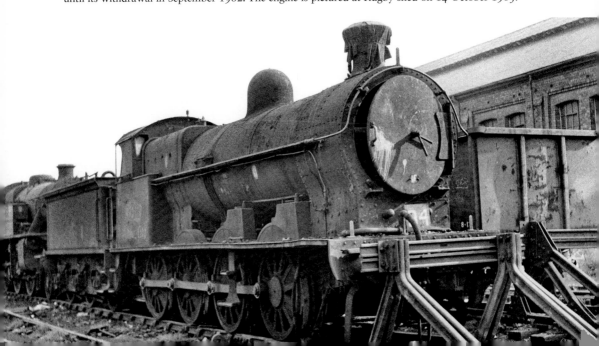

Rugby 48755

The first engine shed serving Rugby was opened by the London & Birmingham Railway in 1838. This was followed by a shed built by the Midland Counties Railway in 1840 and there were further additions to these facilities by both companies over the ensuing years. No. 48755 is seen outside Rugby No. 1 shed, which was built by the LNWR in 1876. The shed was built on the north side of Rugby Midland station and it had twelve roads that were only open from the east end. Ten years later, the company opened another twelve track shed adjacent to Rugby No. 1, known as Rugby No. 2. It had been closed in 1960 and the building was subsequently removed. Stanier 8F no. 48755 was a new addition to Rugby shed, arriving the week before the picture was taken on 14 October 1963. Rugby No. 1 closed to steam in May 1965 and met the same fate as Rugby No. 2. No. 48755 left service in September 1966 from Saltley shed.

Rugby 42063

Photographed at Rugby on 14 October 1963 is Fairburn's Class 4P 2-6-4T locomotive no. 42063. Emerging from Derby Works in December 1950 the locomotive was initially allocated to Stoke. It later went to Watford, Stoke, Chester (Midland), Newton Heath, Southport, Wigan Central and Lancaster Green Ayre. At the time of the photograph it was only days away from withdrawal, and then it was sent to Crewe to be scrapped.

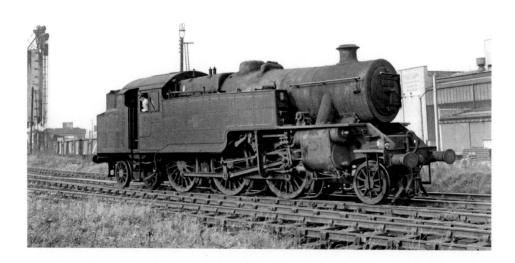

CHAPTER 2

Seaton Station
Northamptonshire to Derby

Seaton Station 84006
Seen replenishing its tank at Seaton station is a BR Standard Class 2 2-6-2T locomotive, no. 84006.
The engine was erected at Crewe Works in August 1953. The water capacity of the Standard Class
2 stood at 1,350 gallons, and it boasted a coal capacity of 3 tons. The first half of the 1960s saw
the engine stored three times as unserviceable, and it spent a total of twenty months out of action.
In October 1965 the locomotive left service and became a victim of the cutter's torch.

Seaton Station 84006

Another view of no. 84006 at Seaton station. The locomotive is on a 'push and pull' service with an unidentified tank engine (probably another Standard Class 2) between Rugby and Peterborough East. Seaton station was opened in June 1851 by the LNWR but was called Seaton and Uppingham and was on the line between Rugby and Stamford. Uppingham was dropped from the name in the latter years of the nineteenth century. The station closed on 6 June 1966 along with the line; both were casualties of the Beeching report.

Seaton Station 84007

Another BR Standard Class 2 photographed from Seaton station. No. 84007 was also built at Crewe Works in August 1953; as with no. 84006, its first allocation was to Burton-on-Trent shed. No. 84007 is with the Rugby to Peterborough East passenger service. Welland Viaduct can be seen to the right of the locomotive; it was built in the late 1870s and is on the Oakham to Kettering line. No. 84007 also had a long period in storage that lasted from September 1962 until December 1963. Withdrawal came in January 1964.

Wellingborough 48625

Stanier 8F 2-8-0 locomotive no. 48625 entered traffic from Brighton Works in April 1943 for the REC. It is pictured next to Wellingborough No. 2 shed, which was a square roundhouse built in 1872 by the Midland Railway. Two other sheds also existed on the shed site, which was located north of Wellingborough station. Another square roundhouse, No. 1 shed, was built by the Midland Railway in 1868 at the north end of the site from No. 2 shed. Between these two sheds was a third that was originally constructed as the coal stage and converted to a shed in the mid-1930s. The locomotive spent the 1950s allocated at the shed, leaving for Cricklewood in July 1960. No. 48625 left service in June 1966 and was scrapped at Cashmore's (Great Bridge).

Wellingborough 92021

Again seen next to Wellingborough No. 2 shed is BR 9F Class 2-10-0 locomotive no. 92021. Construction was carried out at Crewe Works in March 1955 and the engine's first allocation was to Wellingborough shed. It was one of the class fitted with a Crosti boiler; from the look of the engine it appears to be out of service and could be waiting to receive a standard boiler. The locomotive was stored between April 1959 and April 1960 in anticipation of this alteration, and a new boiler had been fitted by June 1960. No. 92021 was in service for several more years before it was sent for scrap in November 1967.

Wellingborough 92020

Another Crosti boiler 9F is seen here at Wellingborough shed. The shed was a main stabling point of the 9F Class in the London Midland Region and was the residence of thirty-seven in early 1960, including all of the Crosti boiler locomotives. The main duty for the 9Fs in the region was hauling coal trains to Brent sidings. However, towards the mid-1960s, diesel locomotives began replacing the 9Fs and the latter found themselves increasingly displaced; Wellingborough had lost its allocation of 9Fs by early 1964. No. 92020 found further work at Kirkby-in-Ashfield, Speke Junction and Birkenhead before withdrawal in October 1967.

Wolverhampton High Level Station 45675

The construction of this LMS Jubilee locomotive, no. 45675 *Hardy*, was carried out by Crewe Works in December 1935. It was among the locomotives built with modifications to the boiler design; these included an increased number of superheater elements, a sloping firebox throatplate, and a dome mounted regulator. *Hardy* has been photographed at Wolverhampton High Level station and is fitted with a Smith-Stone speedometer, dating the picture after September 1960. The engine was allocated to Leeds Holbeck shed from October 1948 until its withdrawal in June 1967.

Leicester 61141 and 61175

Two LNER Thompson B1 Class 4-6-0 locomotives are pictured here at Leicester Belgrave Road station. No. 61141 was built at Vulcan Foundry in April 1947, while no. 61175 entered traffic from there in June 1947. In total, fifty B1s were built at Vulcan Foundry for the LNER with further examples being produced at Gorton, Darlington and the NBLC's works, bringing the class total to 410. No. 61175 was withdrawn from Colwick in December 1963 and scrapped at Doncaster Works.

Leicester 61141

Leicester Belgrave Road station was opened on 2 October 1882 by the Great Northern Railway as the terminus for a branch line from Marefield Junction. Closure to the public came in December 1953, but it remained open for workmen until 29 April 1957 and for summer weekend excursions to Skegness until September 1962. The site has since been redeveloped. No. 61141 was withdrawn from Colwick in July 1965 and sold for scrap.

Basford 61780

GNR Class H3 2-6-0 locomotive was built in July 1921 by Kitson & Co. and designed by Gresley. The H3s (later LNER Class K2) were a modification of GNR Class H2, which had been introduced to replace passenger locomotives that were working on freight services. The H3s had a larger diameter boiler, a higher number of elements in the superheater (changed to the Robinson type) and longer frames. Sixty-five were built by Doncaster, NBLC and Kitson & Co. No. 61780 is photographed working at Basford carriage sidings, which was located to the north of Basford North station on the 'up' side of the Great Central Railway line. The locomotive was allocated to Colwick, having moved from Stratford in October 1952. Withdrawal from the former came in October 1959. Basford North closed in September 1964.

Bulwell 60008

An interesting sight has been captured here at Bulwell Common, Nottingham, on 23 April 1964. Gresley A4 Pacific no. 60008 *Dwight D. Eisenhower* is *en route* from Doncaster to Southampton for shipping to the National Railroad Museum in Green Bay, Wisconsin, USA. The locomotive was built at Doncaster Works in September 1937 as LNER no. 4496 *Golden Shuttle*, changing its name in September 1945. Withdrawal from Peterborough New England shed came in July 1963, and it was restored by Doncaster Works.

Cinderhill 44131

Photographed with a coal train from Cinderhill Colliery is LMS Fowler 4F Class 0-6-0 locomotive no. 44131. The picture was taken at Cinderhill Junction during June 1958 and the train is on the Cinderhill Colliery sidings line to Basford Junction. The design for the locomotive was originated for the Midland Railway as a superheated goods engine. The company classified the locomotives the 3835 Class and 197 were built. After Grouping, the LMS produced more examples with no. 44131 being built at Crewe Works in September 1925. Construction of the class continued until 1941 when 575 had been produced for the LMS. No. 44131 was a Nottingham engine after Nationalisation and later saw moves to Westhouses, Saltley and Bury before it left service in November 1964.

Colwick 64348

Pictured at Colwick shed is a GCR 9J Class (LNER J11) 0-6-0 locomotive, which was designed by J. G. Robinson. The design was a development of earlier GCR engines and incorporated a longer boiler, larger cylinders and increased boiler pressure. A total of 174 were eventually erected at a number of works. This example, no. 64348, was constructed by Beyer, Peacock & Co. in April 1904. It was later fitted with a Robinson type superheater by the GCR in January 1916. In the BR period, the locomotive was allocated to Colwick for only a brief period; it arrived from Retford in January 1959 and was withdrawn from Colwick in March 1960. None of the class have survived into preservation.

East Leake 44936

Passing East Leake station is LMS Black Five no. 44936 heading a London Marylebone express from Nottingham Victoria station during September 1966. This engine was built by Horwich Works in November 1946. It was allocated to Colwick when the picture was taken and only remained there for a few more months before moving to Carlisle Kingmoor in November. No. 44936 operated from Carlisle until August 1967 when it was sent for scrap. East Leake station was opened by the GCR on 15 March 1899 and closed on 5 May 1969.

Gedling 63674

Passing the closed Gedling station with an 'up' coal train is LNER O4 Class 2-8-0 no. 63674. The locomotive was erected by Robert Stephenson & Co. in October 1917 as ROD no. 1655. Construction was carried out for the Railway Operating Division of the Royal Engineers, who placed orders for 325 in February 1917 for use in France during the First World War. The design was based on the GCR Robinson 8K Class. More examples were ordered in 1918 and the total number of engines built for the ROD was 521. After the War, many found themselves in dumps around the country. In 1923 the LNER bought 123 at £2,000 each; one was ROD no. 1655, later LNER no. 6351. A further 148 were in service for the LNER by May 1929. No. 6351 entered service in August 1924 to Scotland after modifications and was classified O4/2. It was rebuilt in May 1947 to O4/8, receiving a B1 type boiler and new cab and chimney. No. 63674 was removed from service in January 1966.

Newark Castle Station 69821

LNER A5 Class 4-6-2T locomotive no. 69821 is depicted at Newark Castle station. The design for the engine came from Robinson and was produced for GCR London suburban passenger services. The first of the class emerged from Gorton Works in March 1911, classified 9N, and this example was constructed at the works in February 1923. Twenty one were in operation when the GCR ordered a further 10 just before Grouping and some of this order never worked a service for the GCR. The LNER later ordered a further 13, which were slightly modified from the GCR engines. No. 69821 left service from Lincoln shed in May 1960 after a three year allocation.

Newark Castle 44585

Fowler 4F Class 0-6-0 no. 44585 was constructed at Derby Works in July 1939. The engines built for the LMS differed from their Midland Railway counterparts due to a few minor alterations. These included changing from right to left hand drive, adopting Ross pop safety valves and reducing the height of the boiler to improve the locomotive's route availability. Newark Castle station was opened by the Midland Railway on 4 August 1846 as Newark station and Castle was added to the title on 25 September 1950. No. 44585 was allocated to Bath at Grouping and by 1950 it was at Nottingham shed. This latter would be its home until September 1960 when its time in service came to an end.

Nottingham Midland Station 70052

BR Britannia Class Pacific locomotive no. 70052 *Firth of Tay* is photographed at Nottingham Midland station with unlined green livery which was applied to the class post-1963. Crewe Works built the engine in August 1954 and it started work from Polmadie shed. Moving to Corkerhill shed in April 1962, it was not until May 1965 that the locomotive received its first English shed allocation to Crewe South. Withdrawal came in April 1967 from Carlisle Kingmoor. Nottingham Midland station was opened on 4 June 1839 in Carrington Street, moving to Station Street on 22 May 1848. The station was known as Nottingham Midland from June 1951 and became Nottingham on 6 May 1970.

Nottingham Victoria 61264

LNER Thompson B1 Class 4-6-0 locomotive no. 61264 was built by the NBLC's Queen's Park
Works in December 1947. The B1 class was built to replace a number of older classes operated by
the LNER; the new engines incorporated a larger number of standard parts than their predecessors
in order to keep maintenance costs down. No. 61264 is seen at Nottingham Victoria station with
a Mablethorpe excursion special. Withdrawal from Colwick came in December 1965, but it saw
further use in departmental stock as a stationary boiler for carriage heating and was renumbered
29. Final withdrawal came in July 1967 and although destined for scrap, no. 61264 managed to
survive into preservation. In 1997 it was returned to working condition and at the present time is
undergoing reconstruction at Crewe.

Nottingham Victoria 70015

BR Britannia Pacific no. 70015 *Apollo* is pictured on the turntable line at the south end of Nottingham Victoria station. Built at Crewe Works, the engine entered traffic in June 1951 to Camden shed. When new, the locomotive was paired with BRI tender no. 774, which had a water capacity of 4,250 gallons and 7 tons of coal. *Apollo* was originally fitted with boiler no. 816, which it carried until replaced by boiler no. 801 from no. 70000 *Britannia* in August 1955. Another change occurred in January 1958 when it received boiler no. 973, originally paired with no. 70025 *Western Star*. No. 70015 *Apollo* left service in August 1967.

Nottingham Victoria 60008

Gresley A4 Pacific no. 60008 *Dwight D. Eisenhower* is seen at Nottingham Victoria station again on its way to Southampton. The locomotive returned to Britain in October 2012 with Canadian resident no. 60010 *Dominion of Canada* for the 75th anniversary celebrations of no. 60022 *Mallard*'s world speed record for a steam locomotive. The station was opened in May 1900 by both the GCR and GNR, but closed on 4 September 1967 and subsequently was demolished. However, the station clock tower is still standing and part of the Victoria shopping centre.

Nottingham Victoria Station 46251

Coronation Class Pacific no. 46251 *City of Nottingham* entered traffic from Crewe Works in June 1944. The locomotive is at Nottingham Victoria station with the RCTS East Midlander special, which went to Eastleigh and Swindon Works on 9 May 1964. Three locomotives were used for the special including no. 46251; the others were Southern Railways Bulleid Light Pacific no. 34038 *Lynton* and SR USA Class no. 30071. No. 46251 took the train from Nottingham Victoria to Didcot and on the return from Swindon Works Junction. The locomotive had little time left in service at this time and was withdrawn in October to be scrapped.

Radcliffe-on-Trent 48538

LMS Stanier 8F 2-8-0 locomotive no. 48538 was erected at Doncaster Works in August 1945 for the REC. The locomotive was fitted with a LMS 3C boiler with a pressure of 225 psi. It had two outside cylinders that were 18½ in. by 28 in. Photographed at Radcliffe-on-Trent with a coal train on the 'up' goods line, no. 48538 left service from Saltley shed in March 1967 and was scrapped at Cashmore's (Great Bridge) scrapyard.

Southwell 58065

Midland Railway 2228 Class 0-4-4T locomotive no. 58065 was erected by Dübs & Co. in February 1892. The class had 165 members that were constructed between 1881 and 1900 to the design of Samuel Johnson. The locomotives were classified 1P by the LMS and only fifty-six survived into the BR era. No. 58065 is pictured at Southwell station with the 'push-and-pull' service to Rolleston Junction. Southwell station was opened by the Midland Railway in July 1847 on a branch line that joined the Lincoln to Nottingham line at Rolleston Junction. Southwell station closed a number of times during its early existence before opening in September 1860 until final closure in June 1959. Rolleston Junction station is still open but has been known as Rolleston since May 1973. No. 58065 left service in November 1959.

Whitchurch GWR 5322

Constructed in August 1917 at Swindon Works, this GWR 4300 Class 2-6-0 locomotive saw service in the First World War before entering traffic for the GWR in 1919. Eleven of these Churchward designed engines were in France hauling munitions and hospital trains during hostilities. By 1932, 342 members of the class were in existence on both passenger and goods services. No. 5322 is seen at Whitchurch station with the 14.05 service to Welshpool. The station was opened by the LNWR on 1 September 1858 as part of the Crewe and Shrewsbury Railway. The engine ceased operating services in April 1964 and was sent for scrap. However, in the late 1960s it went into preservation and after a period of inactivity was returned to service to work at the Didcot Railway Centre.

Burton-on-Trent 41328

No. 41328 was among the last members of the Ivatt Class 2 2-6-2T to be built. It was constructed as part of an order for ten locomotives from Derby Works and entered service in May 1952. These ten were also built with push-and-pull service capabilities; no. 41328 is operating the Burton-on-Trent to Tutbury push-and-pull service, also known as the 'Tutbury Jenny'.

Burton-on-Trent 41328

At the time of this photograph, no. 41328 was allocated to Burton-on-Trent shed having come from Wellingborough, its residence since it was built in February 1959. Burton-on-Trent shed also had another member of the class arrive at the same time, no. 41277, which was also fitted with push-and-pull apparatus. The shed only had one other member of the class reside there, no. 41230, which departed in September 1951. No. 41277 and No. 41328 left in December 1960 and the latter found further work at Southport and Eastleigh before its withdrawal in July 1964.

Chaddesden Sidings 58085

Probably awaiting the cutter's torch is MR 2228 Class 0-4-4T locomotive no. 58085 at Chaddesden sidings near Derby. It was erected by Dübs & Co. in April 1900; the company's Queens Park Works later became part of the NBLC. While in service for BR, the locomotive had allocations at Wellingborough, Leicester, Retford, Nottingham and Lincoln before leaving service in April 1959. It was scrapped by Derby Works during 1960.

Chaddesden Sidings 43930

Fowler 4F 0-6-0 no. 43930, pictured again at Chaddesden sidings. Building occurred at Derby Works in November 1920 and its career ended forty years later in December 1960. The sidings were built alongside the Midland line between Derby and Spondon. Work was carried out preparing the land between 1859 and 1863 and cost around £15,000. Two sorting sidings had been added by the 1870s, as well as wagon repair shops, good offices and a twelve road carriage shed.

Chaddesden Sidings 49418

LNWR Beames G2 Class 0-8-0 no. 49418 was constructed in March 1922 at Crewe Works. At Grouping the locomotive was allocated to Swansea and was later housed at Nuneaton until a move to Stockport Edgeley shed in November 1952. It was withdrawn from the latter in November 1959 and scrapped. Only one member of the class survived into preservation, no. 49395, which has been in operation at the East Lancashire Railway on loan from the National Railway Museum.

Chaddesden Sidings 41120

During the mid-1950s the importance of Chaddesden sidings grew as smaller marshalling sidings were closed and the bulk of the traffic was diverted to the area. However, by the mid-1960s Chaddesden too had declined following a rapid degeneration of the rail freight industry. The majority of the site closed and traffic was diverted to Toton. The site also had the role of storing old locomotives and surplus coaching and wagon stock during this period. LMS Class 4P 4-4-0 Compound locomotive no. 41120 was built at Horwich Works in October 1925 to Fowler's designs. Withdrawal from Llandudno Junction shed came in June 1959; after being stored at various sites it was scrapped at Ward's, Killamarsh, during the last few months of 1960.

Derby D5708

Photographed at Derby, British Railways Class 28 Diesel Electric locomotive no. D5708 was built by Metropolitan-Vickers at their Bowesfield Works in January 1959, as part of an order for twenty by BR. The design was unusual as it utilised a six wheel and four wheel bogie. As with other BR diesel classes at the time, the locomotives were beset by problems and were withdrawn early. D5708 was allocated to Derby shed from new until moved to Barrow in Furness in February 1962. It left service in September 1968 and scrapped, while the last of the class went the following year. D5705 has been preserved.

Derby Shed 41062

LMS Class 4P 4-4-0 Compound locomotive no. 41062 emerged from Derby Works in June 1924. Three other works contributed to the manufacture of the class: Horwich, twenty; NBLC, twenty-five; and Vulcan Foundry, seventy-five. A total of 195 were in operation when the last of the class entered service from Derby Works in 1932. No. 41063 is displaying 21B shed code suggesting that at the time of the picture it was allocated to Bourneville shed. It had arrived there in September 1957 from Sheffield Millhouses shed and left for Derby shed in February 1959. The locomotive left service three months later in May 1959. Behind the engine to the right is the shed coaling stage, which was installed by Henry Lees & Co. in 1936.

Derby Shed 44279

Derby had been served by a number of locomotive sheds over the years with the majority being situated on the south side of Derby Works, which was located on the east side of the lines that ran through the station. The first shed was opened by the Midland Counties Railway in June 1839 and was in use until 1863 when integrated into the works. A number of roundhouses were installed following the opening of the first shed, but these were similarly taken into use by Derby Works. The shed which was open during the BR period was built by the MR in 1890 and was a square building holding two roundhouses. LMS Fowler 4F no. 44279 was no stranger to Derby Works as it had been built there in December 1926. It was a long-term resident at Coalville shed and was condemned while there in January 1964.

Derby Shed 44863

Pictured at Derby shed, LMS Stanier Black Five no. 44863 was constructed as part of Order No. 457 at Crewe Works in January 1945. It was among a number built around this time to feature valve spindle crosshead guides made from fabricated steel. Materials used previously included gunmetal and cast-iron. The motion of no. 44863 and others constructed in this period also featured fluted coupling rods with eccentric rod big ends that were fitted with SKF ball bearings with a brass cover. The locomotive was allocated to Rugby shed for a significant portion of its career, but left there in January 1965 for Bletchley. Derby shed was closed during March 1967 and the site was subsequently cleared. No. 44863 ended its career in May 1967.

Derby Works 58850

North London Railway Class 75 0-6-0T locomotive no. 58850 emerged from Bow Works around 1879-80. The class was designed by J. C. Park to work the company's dock railways and the number produced eventually reached thirty. Later, the class could be found working steeply graded lines in Derbyshire. No. 58850 was the last of the class to be withdrawn in September 1960 from Rowsley shed. Despite the instruction on the side of the tank, the locomotive was preserved by the Bluebell Railway in 1962 after being stored at Derby. It is currently on display awaiting a return to working order.

Derby Works 41168

The LMS 4-4-0 Compounds were a slightly modified version of the MR Compounds that were designed by S. W. Johnson. The difference was that the 7 ft diameter of the driving wheels on the MR locomotives was reduced to 6 ft 9 in. on the LMS engines. Members of the class built during 1925, and later were fitted with left hand drive as it had become standard on LMS locomotives, providing a further variation between the two classes. No. 41168 entered traffic from Vulcan Foundry in October 1925 and the locomotive's removal from service came in July 1961 while at Monument Lane shed. The task of scrapping the engine was carried out at Derby Works and the locomotive was awaiting its fate when pictured on 31 August 1961.

Derby Works 40047

LMS Fowler Class 3P 2-6-2T engine no. 40047 entered service from Derby Works in July 1931. Three batches of the class were built between 1930 and 1932, with the eventual total standing at seventy. No. 40047 had allocations at Bushbury, Walsall, Stoke, Nuneaton and Willesden after Nationalisation. Withdrawal came in November 1959; it was stored for a time at Derby's Klondyke sidings before it was scrapped by Derby Works early in 1960.

Derby Works 47315

Derby Works was opened in 1840 by the North Midland Railway as a repair centre for their locomotives. The works became part of the MR during 1844 and it was not until 1851 that the first locomotive was built there – an 0-6-0 goods locomotive numbered 166. LMS Fowler 3F 0-6-0T no. 47315 was built by W. G. Bagnall in February 1929. The locomotive was one of several of the class that entered service for the Somerset & Dorset Joint Railway and it was given SDJR no. 24. However, the locomotives were not under SDJR ownership for too long, transferring to LMS stock in 1930. No. 47315 left service from Willesden in August 1959.

Derby St Andrew's Sidings 58192

Midland Railway 1357 Class 0-6-0 no. 58192 was erected by Dübs & Co. in 1878 to Johnson's design. The locomotive was built as part of an order for twenty locomotives from the company, and this followed a batch of thirty that was completed in 1875. The new engines differed from earlier examples built by Dübs and other manufacturers in their larger diameter driving wheels; from 4 ft 10 in. on the older engines, to 5 ft 2 in. on the new ones. The cost of construction was £2,274. Withdrawal for no. 58192 came in December 1958 and it was scrapped at Doncaster Works in 1960.

Derby St Andrew's Sidings 41102

Another LMS 4-4-0 Compound, no. 41102, pictured at Derby St Andrew's sidings. Erected at Derby Works in October 1925, it entered service as LMS no. 1102. The engine had numerous allocations after Nationalisation and was withdrawn from Derby in December 1958. It was stored for a time in St Andrew's sidings before scrapping at Doncaster Works.

Derby St Andrew's Sidings 58157

The goods sidings were built pre-1870 by the LNWR at the south end of Derby station on the north side of the Birmingham line. This MR 1142 Class Johnson 0-6-0 engine no. 58157 was the forerunner of the 1357 Class locomotive no. 58192, also seen at Derby. Assembly of the engine was carried out by Beyer, Peacock & Co. in April 1876 and it was part of the initial order for 120 given to four works. The cost was slightly higher than charged by Dübs & Co. and stood at £2,650 per engine. November 1958 was the locomotive's final month in service.

Derby St Andrew's Sidings 47249

MR Johnson 2441 Class 0-6-0T locomotive no. 47249 was erected at Vulcan Foundry in June 1902 and was one of sixty from there. The class was not originally constructed with Belpaire fireboxes, they were fitted from 1919 under the direction of Fowler. The locomotive is seen fitted with condensing apparatus suggesting it operated at some time in the London area. No. 47429 is displaying the 56E shed code, denoting Sowerby Bridge, which was the engine's last allocation. It left service in November 1958.

Derby St Andrew's Sidings 41090

The LNWR goods wharf consisted of a large goods warehouse, six tracks and sidings. At Grouping it dealt with goods from former LNWR and North Staffordshire Railway lines and distributed them around the Derby area. In 1924 the name was changed from Derby Station Goods to Derby St Andrew's, as the yard was adjacent to a church of the same name. After Nationalisation the goods station declined and the site fell into disuse and now forms part of the station's car park. LMS Fowler Compound no. 41090 was built at Derby Works in July 1925 and was withdrawn in December 1958.

Derby St Andrew's Sidings 58225

MR Johnson 1357 Class, later LMS Class 2F 0-6-0 locomotive no. 58225 was built by Beyer, Peacock & Co. in October 1883. The number of tubes in the boiler differed between all the makers and this locomotive would have originally carried a boiler with 205 1¾ in. tubes giving a heating surface of 1,032 sq. ft. After Nationalisation the locomotive was allocated to Sheffield Millhouses shed and was withdrawn from there in December 1958. The engine was stored at Derby for a time in mid- to late 1960 before being transported to Crewe Works to meet the cutter's torch.

CHAPTER 3

Crewe Works to Chester

Crewe Works CD7
Pictured at Crewe Works is CD7, a LNWR Special Tank 0-6-0ST locomotive. The design was originally conceived by J. Ramsbottom who built twenty locomotives before it was modified by F. W. Webb, resulting in a further 235. The main difference between the two designs was that Ramsbottom used iron frames whereas Webb used steel. Construction was carried out by Crewe Works but the date is unknown. Many of the locomotives were utilised at Wolverton Carriage and Wagon Works, as was the case with this example. Withdrawal for the locomotive came in November 1959 and it was cut up at Crewe. Seen behind CD7 is Bury Tram locomotive no. 84.

Crewe Works 46154

Pictured shortly after it was taken out of the south Erecting Shop at Crewe Works is LMS Royal Scot no. 46154 *The Hussar*, built by Derby Works in July 1930. The photograph dates from April 1959 when the locomotive was at Crewe for light intermediate repairs, which started at the end of February and were completed by the start of April. However, the locomotive returned twice to works in April and it was the end of the month before normal duties were resumed. At this time the locomotive was allocated to Camden, but a month was spent operating from Kentish Town shed from May before returning to Camden. No. 46154's time in service came to an end in December 1962 and it was broken up at Crewe.

Opposite above: Crewe Works 45639

On the left, photographed at Crewe Works with a couple of Standard Class 7 Pacific locomotives, is LMS Stanier Jubilee Class 4-6-0 no. 45639 *Raleigh*. The engine emerged from the works in December 1934 and its first allocation was to Crewe North shed. The locomotive was not named until June 1936 when the plates were fitted at Derby Works. The 55A on the smokebox door indicates allocation to Leeds Holbeck shed, which was a long-term residence for the locomotive. It arrived there in July 1951 and stayed until withdrawal in September 1963, returning to Crewe Works to be scrapped.

Opposite below: Crewe Works 45674

LMS Stanier Jubilee no. 45674 *Duncan* is outside the works' paint shop awaiting attention in April 1959. While at the works the locomotive was fitted with AWS (Automatic Warning System) apparatus; it was among the earliest members of the class to be fitted thus. The first Jubilee to be equipped was no. 45633 *Trans-Jordan* in January 1959. No. 45674 did not have a long distance to return to service after it had finished at the works as it was a Crewe North engine at the time of the picture. The engine was condemned in October 1964 and it was cut up at A. Draper's Kingston upon Hull scrapyard.

Crewe Works CD6

Another Wolverton Carriage and Wagon Works shunting locomotive is pictured at Crewe Works waiting to become another casualty of the diesel takeover. The LNWR Special Tanks had driving wheels of 4 ft 5½ in. diameter, a boiler of 4 ft 5¾ in. diameter by 10 ft 5¼ in. long, and a pressure of 150 psi. They had two cylinders measuring 17 in. diameter by 24 in. stroke, and the total weight of the locomotive was 34 tons 10 cwt. Only the members of the class employed at Wolverton survived after Nationalisation, and the last locomotive in normal service was withdrawn in 1941.

Crewe Works 70051

BR Britannia Pacific no. 70051 *Firth of Forth* entered traffic from Crewe Works in August 1954. The engine returned to Crewe for light intermediate maintenance in March 1960, when it had run nearly 90,000 miles since its previous general overhaul. No. 70051 would accumulate only 75,000 miles before returning to the works for heavy intermediate repairs between April/May 1962. The average mileage between visits to the works for the Britannia Class was 100,000-125,000 miles. Crewe was originally given the sole responsibility of major overhauls for the class, but this task was later extended to include Doncaster and Swindon with other regional works involved in the general maintenance. Crewe regained sole responsibility again in June 1962. *Firth of Forth* was withdrawn in December 1967.

Crewe Works 51412

Photographed shunting in the works yard is Lancashire & Yorkshire Railway Class 23 0-6-0ST locomotive no. 51412. The engine was built by Beyer, Peacock & Co. in September 1895 as L&YR no. 598, to the design of J. Aspinall, who utilised components from previously constructed 0-6-0 tender locomotives to create new saddletank engines. A number of the L&YR Class 23s worked shunting duties at Crewe along with a contingent of L&YR Class 27s. These were later superseded by LMS 3F tanks when the L&YR locomotives became life-expired. No. 51412 survived until September 1962 and was scrapped on site.

Crewe Works 42654

LMS Stanier 2-6-4T Class 4P locomotive no. 42654 emerged from Derby Works in January 1941. Manufacture of the class commenced in 1935 and did not cease until 1943 when 206 were in existence. Two works were involved in their construction; NBLC (73) and Derby (133). The basis for the design was Stanier's 2-6-4T with three cylinders, built in 1935, but the new engines were changed by reducing the number of cylinders to two and increasing the cylinder size from 16 in. by 26 in. to $19^5/8$ in. by 26 in. No. 42654 was withdrawn from Bolton shed, where it had been a long-term resident, in November 1964.

Crewe Works 46164

LMS Royal Scot no. 46164 *The Artists' Rifleman* is seen outside the erecting shop in April 1959 after completing heavy intermediate repairs. Derby Works carried out the locomotive's construction in September 1930 at a cost of nearly £6,500. In the early 1930s, after experiments with various types of smoke deflectors, the class began to be fitted with straight plates; LMS no. 6164 received them in January 1932. It was fitted with curved deflectors in January 1950, nearly eighteen months before it had the taper 102A boiler fitted in June 1951. The locomotive left service from Sheffield Darnall shed in December 1962.

Crewe Works 46100

Another Royal Scot in the erecting shop yard during April 1959 was the first locomotive in the class numbering scheme, no. 46100 *Royal Scot*. The NBLC's Queens Park Works had the task of erecting the locomotive and it was officially in service by August 1927. The construction cost the LMS £7,740. *Royal Scot* was at Crewe for light intermediate maintenance at the time of this photograph and it would re-enter traffic at the start of May. The locomotive left service during October 1962 and was preserved; it is currently owned by the Royal Scot Locomotive and General Trust.

Crewe Works 41288

This Ivatt Class 2 2-6-2T engine was built at Crewe Works in December 1950 as part of a batch fitted with push-and-pull equipment. It has been photographed outside the works paint shop, with the job seemingly completed. The paint shop was located at the east end of Crewe Works. The wheel and brass finishing shops were immediately to the west on the north and south sides of the lines to the paint shop. This part of the site has now been cleared and is occupied by housing and a supermarket. No. 41288 left service from Warrington Dallam shed in October 1962.

Crewe Works 46257

LMS Stanier Coronation Pacific no. 46257 *City of Salford* was the last of the class to be built. It emerged from Crewe Works in May 1948 and was allocated to Camden shed. The locomotive incorporated a number of modifications when built, including roller bearings, improved axlebox lining, altered cab sides and trailing truck. No. 46257 was a regular visitor to Crewe Works during 1959, notching up four visits. The first came in January for a heavy general and it was not completed until 13 March. It returned on the 22nd and did not leave again until the end of April. Mid-July saw no. 46257 back for a non-classified, but in the intervening time it had amassed around 19,000 miles so it was probably ready for some attention. The last visit came at the start of September and it was on site for forty-three days. Withdrawal came in September 1964.

Crewe North 46252

Photographed inside the semi-roundhouse at Crewe North shed is LMS Stanier Coronation Pacific no. 46252 *City of Leicester*. The date is March 1960 and the locomotive is only three months away from being transferred to Carlisle Upperby shed; the locomotive had been resident at Crewe North since September 1956. Construction of *City of Leicester* was carried out at Crewe Works in April 1944 and it was the last of four erected during the year; none of these engines were streamlined. No. 46252 left service at the start of June 1963 after six months in storage.

Opposite above: Crewe Works 42674

Operations at Crewe Works commenced in 1843 under the direction of the Grand Junction Railway; the first locomotive, a 2-2-2, was built in October of that year. In 1846 the GJR became a constituent of the LNWR and the works then operated for the latter company. In the early 1860s the site was expanded and in 1866 the 1,000th locomotive was built – no. 613, a DX Class 0-6-0. LMS Fairburn Class 4P 2-6-4T no. 42674 emerged from Derby in April 1945. It was withdrawn from Stoke shed in November 1962.

Opposite below: Crewe Works 45591

The early 1900s saw the 4,000th locomotive constructed at Crewe Works. The site was further expanded and reorganised, with the last major addition to the site being no. 10 erecting shop, which was added in 1926. At its peak the works covered 137 acres and employed around 8,500 people. Despite diversifying into diesel locomotive construction and producing High Speed Train power cars, the works declined, and in the mid-1980s part of the site was sold for redevelopment. The remaining site was acquired by Bombardier in 2001. The focus of the works is now maintenance rather than construction, but at the present time its future remains uncertain. LMS Jubilee no. 45591 *Udaipur* has been photographed in front of the tender shop during March 1960 and is seen in a pink primer before being repainted. It was condemned in October 1963.

Crewe North 45595

The engine is pictured again in Crewe North semi-roundhouse, but the date is now September 1964. The application of the electrification warning line on the side of the cab would have been a new addition for the locomotive as the prohibition had only started from the first of the month. The semi-roundhouse was constructed by BR in 1950 and it contained twelve tracks. It replaced a twelve track straight shed constructed in 1891 and used by engines waiting to enter the works. The locomotive, LMS Jubilee no. 45595 *Southern Rhodesia*, was built by the NBLC's Queens Park Works during January 1935. It had numerous allocations to Crewe North during its service life and began its final stay in June 1959. At the end of September 1964 it was transferred on loan to Llandudno Junction and left service in January 1965.

Crewe North 42963

The LMS Stanier 2-6-0 locomotives were a modification of the Hughes 'Crab' design and forty were constructed to enhanced specifications; no. 42963 emerged from Crewe Works in December 1933. The main differences were the employment of taper boilers and horizontal cylinders. After Nationalisation no. 42963 was allocated to Crewe North from September 1954 and spent three months on loan to Newton Heath during the allocation. The engine defected to Crewe South in September 1961 and was not withdrawn until July 1966 from Wigan Springs Bank shed.

Crewe North 46155

Pictured after coming off the 70 ft turntable (installed by BR in 1950) and at its main home during the BR period, is LMS Royal Scot no. 46155 *The Lancer*. The electrification warning stripe on the cab indicates the picture was taken after September 1964 when the locomotive was a month away from a transfer to Carlisle Kingmoor shed. It only survived a further two months before it was withdrawn for scrapping, which was carried out by the Shipbreaking Co., Troon. No. 46155 *The Lancer* is on a section of track located to the east side of the semi-roundhouse and stands next to BR Standard Class 7 Pacific no. 70017 *Arrow*.

Crewe North 45552

LMS no. 5552 was the first locomotive of the Jubilee class to be built in May 1934 at Crewe Works. A further four locomotives followed it into service during the next two months, but these, along with further examples, proved to be difficult to operate efficiently. Modifications were subsequently made to the boilers fitted to no. 5642 (built December 1934 at Crewe) onwards in an attempt to improve their steaming. Then, in 1935, to celebrate the Silver Jubilee of King George VI and Queen Mary, a locomotive was chosen to be named after this occasion. Due to the bad performance of the earlier locomotives, no. 5552 was not chosen for this honour, but instead it was no. 5642, and a permanent switch of identities occurred. No. 5552 *Silver Jubilee* had a special livery applied consisting of gloss black with chrome highlights with chrome numbers; certainly a neater appearance than presented here.

Crewe North 70019

Pictured on the cusp of Crewe North shed's closure is BR Britannia Pacific no. 70019 *Lightning*, built at the town's works in June 1951. The picture dates from March 1965 and closure to steam locomotives came in May. No. 70017 *Lightning* was withdrawn the following March. The first shed at Crewe was opened on the site during the late 1830s by the GJR. It had one track and was made from timber. The LNWR upgraded the facilities in the early 1850s by replacing the GJR and a Chester & Crewe Railway shed with an eight track dead-end shed and a new coal stage; two twelve track straight sheds followed in 1865 and 1868. The coal facilities were upgraded in 1909 to a mechanical coaler, which was replaced by BR in 1953 by a 200 ton coaler to the north-west of the original one.

Crewe North 46256

The LNWR eight track shed at Crewe North was demolished in 1897 to facilitate improvements to Crewe station. The 1868 twelve track shed was reduced in size to four roads in 1950 to allow the twelve track semi-roundhouse to be added on the west side of the site. When the shed closed, the site was cleared and part of the land later became Crewe station car park, while some of the site is unoccupied. LMS Coronation Pacific no. 46256 *Sir William Stanier F.R.S.* was built at Crewe in December 1947 and had the LMS lined black livery was applied when it entered traffic. It subsequently had BR lined black applied as well as the company's blue and green. The final application was the LMS lined maroon, which was first applied in May 1958. The locomotive left service in October 1964, as did the remaining members of the class.

Crewe South 47354

Seen in the vicinity of Crewe South shed is LMS Class 3F 0-6-0T locomotive no. 47354. Construction was carried out by the NBLC's Queens Park Works in July 1926 and it originally carried no. 16437. In *LMS Locomotive Profiles No. 14 – The Standard Class 3 Goods Tank Engines* the cost of the locomotives built by the NBLC is given as £3,368 each, which was slightly more than the price of the first fifty. The other locomotives ordered in the 1926 building programme came from Vulcan Foundry, who charged £3,300 a locomotive, Bagnall and Co. who charged £3,343, and Hunslet Engine Co. who charged £3,413. No. 47354 had a four year allocation to Crewe South, arriving in November 1960 and leaving in October 1964, after withdrawal, to be broken up.

Crewe South 78007

This broadside view of BR Standard Class 2 2-6-0 no. 78007 was taken while the locomotive was outside Crewe South shed. A development of the LMS Ivatt Class Two 2-6-0s, construction of BR Standard Class 2s began in 1952 and the first entered traffic in December; no. 78007 appeared in March 1953. Darlington produced all of the engines in the class; the last one was turned out as 1956 drew to a close. From Crewe South the Standard Class 2s worked shunting duties and local freight services; a total of nine were allocated to the shed during the second half of the early 1960s. No. 78007 arrived in June 1964 and left in March 1965. It finished its operational life at Bolton and was axed in May 1967.

Crewe South 48158

Two workhorses of the London Midland region, a Stanier 8F and a Stanier Black Five, are waiting to start their next duty at Crewe South shed. No. 48158 was built at Crewe Works in January 1943 and judging from its appearance it was a recent visitor to works. At the time of the photograph, the engine was allocated to 55A – Leeds Holbeck shed, and was a long-term resident there, having seen in Nationalisation at Nottingham. The former did not see a large number of 8Fs, but it had a batch of permanent residents – 48104, 48157, 48283, 48399, 48454 and 48542 – who saw their last days there. No. 48158 left service in September 1967.

Crewe South GWR 6822

The GWR Collett Grange Class 4-6-0s were envisaged at the start of the twentieth century by G. J. Churchward, but the idea came to nothing. The plans were then resurrected by Collett who changed the design of the cab and brought it up to modern standards. Eighty of the class were constructed, all at Swindon, between 1936 and 1939; no. 6822 *Manton Grange* emerged from there in January 1937. *Manton Grange* was a Bristol Barrow Road engine when pictured; it was there from June 1964 for only three months as withdrawal claimed it in September. Crewe South was used as a service point for GWR locomotives after the GWR shed at Crewe closed in June 1963.

Crewe South Unidentified

A numberless Ivatt Class 4 2-6-0 locomotive stands outside Crewe South shed on 24 September 1967. The shed was home to a large contingent of the class towards the end of steam operations and closure came on 6 November 1967, shortly after the picture was taken. Built by the LNWR in October 1897, the shed was a twelve track through-road building located to the south of Crewe station between the west coast main line and Stafford line. BR rebuilt the shed in 1959, providing cover for eight tracks but leaving four open to the elements.

Crewe Station 45552

Running light in the area around Crewe station is LMS Jubilee no. 45552 *Silver Jubilee*. The locomotive had two spells at Crewe North; the first was on loan from Longsight shed in May 1949 before the transfer became permanent towards the end of June. It left for Carlisle Upperby in April 1950 and after a few more moves returned to Crewe North in June 1961. Crewe North was a home to many of the class and it saw 166 of the 191 Jubilees during their time in service. From the shed they could work to places such as Birmingham, Carlisle, Leeds, Liverpool and London on express passenger, fish, parcels, freight and newspaper diagrams. No. 45552 was withdrawn in September 1964 from the shed and was probably not far away from its ultimate fate at the time of the picture.

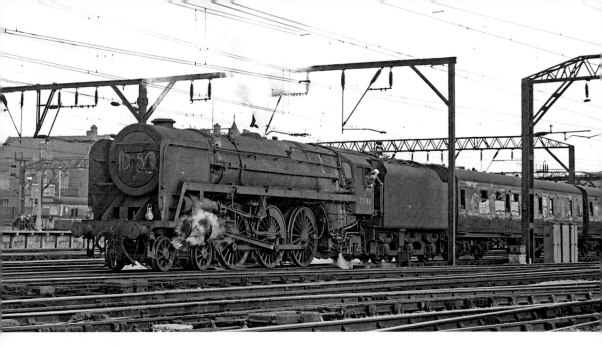

Crewe Station 70046

BR Standard 7 Pacific no. 70046 entered traffic towards the end of June 1954. However, a name was not given to the engine until September 1959, when it acquired *Anzac*. The nameplates are missing in this picture as was the case with many of the class during the last gasp of steam operations. Only one member of the class never carried a name – no. 70047. *Anzac* was paired with a BRID tender, no. 980, when it was built, but it later switched tenders with no. 70045 *Lord Rowallan* in June 1962, then carrying tender no. 979. The BRID had straight sides that created extra space, increasing the capacity to about 9 tons of coal, but with a reduced water capacity to 4,725 gallons. The locomotive was withdrawn in July 1967.

Crewe Station 45105

From the condition of LMS Stanier Black Five no. 45105, it appears to be ex-works when this image was captured on 6 April 1957. From additional pictures taken by Bill at the same time we learn the engine is heading a convoy of other locomotives in a similar condition. Behind it is War Department 2-8-0 'Austerity' no. 90576, and out of shot is LMS Stanier 'Princess Royal' Pacific Class no. 46212 *Duchess of Kent*, all being shunted by an unidentified 0-6-0 (also out of view). They are seen at the north end of Crewe station and are possibly being taken to Crewe North shed for running in before heading back to their home depots. For no. 45105 and for no. 90576, this was Newton Heath shed, but no. 46212 was heading home as it was a Crewe North engine. No. 45105 was removed from service in October 1966.

Crewe Station 42319

Locomotive no. 42319, a member of the LMS Fowler 2-6-4T 4P Class, has been pictured leaving the north end of Crewe station with an unidentified passenger service. All of the class were built at Derby Works and this example was produced during April 1928; the first had entered traffic in December 1927. The last appeared in January 1934 and brought the class total to 125. When this picture was taken on 6 April 1957, the locomotive was allocated to Manchester Longsight shed, but would transfer to Macclesfield in October. No. 42319 was withdrawn in October 1963 from Carnforth shed.

Crewe Station 46162

At the north end of Crewe station is LMS Royal Scot no. 46162 *Queen's Westminster Rifleman*. The locomotive was constructed at Derby Works in September 1930 and allocated to Holyhead shed. When this scene was captured on 6 April 1957, the locomotive was allocated to Carlisle Upperby but would move to Kentish Town in late 1959. It visited Carlisle Upperby and Kingmoor in 1962 before its final allocation to Crewe North in October 1963. It left service in May 1964 and was scrapped by J. N. Connell, Coatbridge.

Crewe Station 41229

Crewe station was opened by the GJR on 4 July 1837 and consisted of only one platform, but was extended to two in 1840. The 1860s saw the station redeveloped and extended as its importance on the west coast route increased. Ivatt Class 2MT 2-6-2 locomotive no. 41229 was built at Crewe Works in October 1948 and was the last of the class to be produced until August the following year. Again the picture was taken on 6 April 1957 and the engine was Crewe North allocated. It was withdrawn in November 1966.

Crewe Station 78030

BR Standard Class 2 no. 78030 has quite an audience looking on from Crewe station's north end footbridge on 6 April 1957. The footbridge was a popular spot for local enthusiasts to view the comings and goings at the station and the movement of traffic between the sheds and works. No. 78030 was constructed in September 1954 and started its career at Preston shed. In April 1956 it moved to Crewe North and for a long time was the only member of the class at the shed. It was employed on shunting and pilot duties around the station and might be moving coaching stock in the picture. No. 78030 could also be found on passenger duties on the Crewe to Wellington branch line. It relocated to Crewe South in October 1964 and was sent to the cutters torch the following October.

Crewe Station 46236

Crewe station saw further expansion in the early years of the twentieth century as more platforms were added. The facilities remained little altered until the electrification scheme which lasted from 1959 to 1974. The station was not changed again until the mid-1980s when major renovations were carried out. No. 46236 *City of Bradford* is on the 'Royal Scot' service on 6 April 1957. Withdrawal for the locomotive came in March 1964 and it was dismantled at Crewe.

Saltney Junction 44831

Pictured in the Saltney Junction area (where the GWR line met the LNWR Chester – Holyhead line) is LMS Stanier Black Five no. 44831. The locomotive was built by Crewe Works in August 1944 with a number of modified features from members of the class constructed previously. These changes included increased frame thickness, use of hornblocks, link and pin cross stays at the horns, and the discontinued use of wooden frames for the cab windows. No. 44831 spent the 1950s allocated to Rugby and left for Stoke in August 1962. Further allocations followed to Holyhead, Chester and Wigan. It was withdrawn during November 1967.

Winsford Sidings 49157

Crewe Works built this LNWR G1 Class 0-8-0 locomotive no. 49157 in February 1912 to the design of Charles Bowen Cooke. A total of 170 new locomotives were constructed to the design while a further 278 engines were rebuilt by both the LNWR and LMS to the class specifications. No. 49157 was itself rebuilt in August 1939 to become part of Class G2A. The locomotive was withdrawn from Pontypool Road shed in January 1959 and stored at Winsford sidings until transported to Cashmore's (Great Bridge) scrapyard and dismantled there during the early part of 1960.

Winsford Sidings 41945

Winsford sidings were on the Winsford & Over branch line, which left the Chester – Manchester line at Winsford Junction. The track was opened by the Cheshire Lines Committee in the mid-1870s. LMS 3P Class 4-4-2T locomotive no. 41945 is pictured at Winsford sidings after it was withdrawn in February 1959. The design for the locomotive was based on the London, Tilbury & Southend Railway Class 73, which was planned by Thomas Whitelegg. These were in turn a development of the LTSR Class 37. Only four of the Class 73s were built by the LTSR; ten were ordered by the MR, but they entered service for the LMS. The latter company ordered another five in 1925 and further batches of ten were constructed in 1927 and 1930. No. 41945 entered service in June 1927 from Derby Works.

Winsford Sidings 41982

Another LTSR locomotive, but this time it is a Class 69 0-6-2T engine. No. 41982 was erected by the NBLC in June 1903 as LTSR no. 71 *Wakering*. It was part of the initial four built to the design of Whitelegg; eventually fourteen were constructed in total. The locomotives had 5 ft 3 in. diameter driving wheels, two cylinders measuring 18 in. by 26 in., and Stephenson valve gear. After Nationalisation the locomotive was allocated to Plaistow and Tilbury. It was withdrawn from the former in March 1959 and stored at Winsford before being cut by Hayes/Bird's scrapyard in Bridgend.

Chester 44696

Construction of the last forty Black Fives was authorised by the LMS in October 1947, but all entered service for British Railways. Their construction was carried out by Crewe and Horwich Works, with the latter being the birthplace of no. 44696. It was the penultimate member of the class to enter traffic in November 1950. The superheaters on the locomotives built after Nationalisation were modified by BR to have standard return loop elements, which were 1 3/8 in. diameter and 9 swg. The locomotives of the final batch built at Horwich Works were also fitted with Timken roller bearings, but only on the driving axle. No. 44696 was photographed at Chester station on 22 August 1964, and was a Stockport Edgeley shed resident at this time. It left service from Newton Heath shed in May 1967.

Chester 44708

This photograph was taken on 22 August 1964 from Hoole Lane Bridge at Chester. Black Five no. 44708 has left the east end of Chester station and is taking the Manchester line, while to the left is the line to Crewe. No. 44708 was built in September 1948 at Horwich Works. It is seen with the altered top-feed arrangement where the apparatus has been moved to the first barrel ring. This was done to ease maintenance and reduce problems encountered when it was in use. The top-feed also has the new style clackbox as the setscrews are covered by the 'top hat' fairing. No. 44708 was a Patricroft engine at this time, but would move to Trafford Park in November. It was withdrawn from there in January 1968.

Chester 48446

Stanier 8F 2-8-0 no. 48446 was built by Swindon Works in July 1944. A total of eighty were produced there between June 1943 and July 1945, and taken into GWR stock on loan from the LMS. While on the GWR, the locomotive was allocated to Reading shed, but it was returned to the LMS in April 1947. Since that time the locomotive has acquired a numberplate on the smokebox door, which it would not have had on the GWR as the company applied the number to the bufferbeam. No. 48446 was withdrawn in July 1965, almost a year after this image was captured.

Chester 73133

BR Standard Class 5 4-6-0 locomotive no. 73133 has been pictured in the area around Chester station on 22 August 1964. The design for the class was essentially based on the Black Fives of the LMS, but with slightly larger driving wheels. A total of 172 were constructed to the design at Derby and Doncaster Works. This example emerged from Derby Works during September 1956 and was one of thirty built with British-Caprotti valve gear. The locomotive was at Patricroft shed from September 1958, leaving Shrewsbury – its shed from new. From Patricroft the engine would have worked to Liverpool, north Wales and Yorkshire. It left service in June 1968.

Chester 42963

Photographed running light at the west end of Chester station and passing under Hoole Way bridge is LMS Stanier 2-6-0 no. 42963. In the distance, behind the tender, is Chester shed, which closed to steam in 1960 and later became a DMU depot. No. 42963 was built in December 1933 as no. 13263, and attached to a Fowler 3,500 gallon tender with a coal capacity of 5 tons. Allocated to Wigan Springs Branch shed at this time, the engine would leave service from there in July 1966.

Chester 45699

LMS Stanier Jubilee 4-6-0 no. 45699 *Galatea* was constructed by Crewe Works in April 1936. The intention was for the locomotive to enter traffic with a Stanier 4,000 gallon tender; however, the Royal Scot Class needed the larger capacity Stanier tenders and a transfer was initiated. Jubilees that were in traffic and engines that were being built lost their tenders and received Fowler 3,500 gallon tenders from the Royal Scots. As LMS no. 5699, the locomotive was given tender no. 3917 from engine no. 6118 *Royal Welch Fusilier*, with tender no. 9333 going the other way. A further exchange was instigated when a number of 4F 0-6-0s were built with Stanier 4,000 gallon tenders, so the Fowler tenders from the Jubilees could be substituted. *Galatea* was again involved and received tender no. 9776 in April 1940.

Chester 70026

This image was taken at the east end of Chester station and shows BR Britannia Class Pacific no. 70026 *Polar Star* passing through on 22 August 1964 with an unidentified passenger service. The locomotive entered traffic in October 1952 to Cardiff Canton shed. In November 1955 *Polar Star* was involved in a serious derailment at Milton while hauling a Treherbert to Paddington excursion; tragically, ten people were killed. It was subsequently noted by the enquiry that the smoke deflector handrails were a contributing factor as they partially obscured the driver's view. To remedy this, the handrails were replaced by hand holes of varying types; no. 70026 was modified in the Western Region style. The engine continued in service until January 1967.

Chester 42482

Two stations originally existed in Chester; one was opened by the Birkenhead, Lancashire & Cheshire Junction Railway in September 1840, while the other was operated by the Chester & Crewe Railway, with services commencing in October 1840. Both were replaced by a joint station involving the former company, LNWR and Chester & Holyhead Railway in 1848, later falling under the direction of the LNWR and GWR. LMS Stanier 4P 2-6-4T locomotive no. 42482 was built at Derby Works in February 1937. After an initial batch of the class was built, subsequent locomotive's boilers were changed to include a separate dome and top-feed arrangement. The boilers were tapered and classified 4C, working at 200 psi. The engine was withdrawn from Chester shed in April 1965.

Chester 46230

A resplendent-looking LMS Stanier Coronation Pacific has been pictured at Chester station. No. 46230 *Duchess of Buccleuch* was erected at Crewe Works in June 1938 and had the distinction of being the first of the class to appear without being streamlined; the preceding five 'Duchesses' had been built with streamlining. No. 46230 received a double chimney in October 1940 and smoke deflectors in September 1946. A long-term Polmadie resident from February 1940, the engine was withdrawn during November 1963 after a period in storage.

CHAPTER 4

Northwich to Carlisle

Northwich 63743

Seen at the ash pits at Northwich shed is GCR Robinson 8K Class 2-8-0 no. 63743, which was built by the NBLC's Hyde Park Works in August 1912 and numbered 1206. It appeared with a Robinson 24 element superheater, but the apparatus was standardised on the class to 22 elements from 1916. After Grouping, the locomotive became no. 6206, receiving its number in February 1925. The LNER made some modifications to the engines and two seen here are the shorter chimney and the Gresley anti-vacuum valve behind it. The engine is still fitted with a Belpaire firebox; many members of the class had theirs replaced by round-topped fireboxes. No. 63743 was withdrawn in June 1962.

Northwich 63775

A ROD-built example of Robinson's 8K Class, later LNER O4 Class, is pictured adjacent to no. 63743 at Northwich shed. No. 63775 was constructed by the NBLC's Queens Park Works during April 1918 and allocated ROD no. 1869. The locomotive was amongst the final hundred bought by the LNER in 1927 from the dumps at Queensferry, Gretna and Morecambe, and entered service in December as no. 6586. It was rebuilt by Gresley to class part seven in August 1940, which included changing the boiler to diagram 15D. It was withdrawn in March 1962.

Rowsley 58850

NLR Class 75 locomotive no. 58850 pauses at its long-term home, Rowsley shed. The facilities were opened by the LMS in 1924 to the south of Rowsley station. The building had four tracks, and other amenities included a water tank, turntable and coal stage. The first shed, serving the first station at Rowsley, was opened by the Manchester, Buxton & Midland Junction Railway during 1849 and was operational until its replacement in 1880 by a shed opened by the MR. The LMS shed was closed at the end of April 1964 and demolished. The station was closed in 1967 and the line between Rowsley and Matlock was then lifted. Part of the line has subsequently re-opened as a heritage railway operated by Peak Rail.

Heaton Mersey 48191

LMS Stanier 8F 2-8-0 no. 48191 is on the turntable at Heaton Mersey shed, Stockport. Construction of the locomotive was carried out by the NBLC in May 1942. The locomotive displays a star on the cab side, indicating that it is suitable for fast freight and passenger services as the reciprocating balance was 50 per cent. Some of the class had 40 per cent reciprocating balance or none at all (modified to 40 per cent by 1962), and these were only suitable for slower duties as speeds of over 40 mph caused them to become unstable.

Heaton Mersey 48191

Heaton Mersey shed was opened by the Chester Lines Committee in 1889 and it had eight roads. The turntable was originally 50 ft, but in 1952 it was upgraded to 70 ft and was moved to the position seen here. The shed had a strong link with the 8Fs, and after Nationalisation, it saw 102 members of the class for varying periods. No. 48191 was a long-term resident arriving in March 1957 and leaving in May 1968 for Rose Grove shed, Burnley. It was withdrawn from the latter in August 1968. Heaton Mersey shed closed to steam in May 1968; the site has since been cleared and has become an industrial estate.

Newton Heath 48678

Newton Heath shed was a large facility located to the west of the station of the same name. Both were opened by the Lancashire & Yorkshire Railway, but the shed was the later addition to the area, being brought into use during 1876. Twenty-four roads were contained in the brick-built structure. No. 48678 is in the shed yard with two other 8Fs visible to the left and behind the engine. No. 48678 was constructed at Brighton Works in June 1944 for the REC. In November 1946 the locomotive was fitted with manual blowdown equipment as part of experiments to reduce problems with the top-feed. However, the apparatus did not provide an adequate solution and the trials were discontinued in the early 1950s. No. 48678 was withdrawn in June 1968 from Newton Heath; it had been allocated there for six months.

Manchester Victoria 45420

This Armstrong Whitworth-built LMS Stanier Black Five entered traffic in October 1937. It was photographed at Manchester Victoria station in the mid- to late 1960s when it was allocated to Newton Heath shed. Arriving there in June 1965, it was withdrawn in June 1968. At the outset the locomotive was attached to a Mark Two tender with a capacity of 9 tons of coal and 4,000 gallons of water, but it later received a Mark One tender from November 1943.

Bolton 49662

The LMS Fowler 7F Class 0-8-0 locomotives were a progression of the LNWR 0-8-0s, with a number of modifications over their predecessors. These included new frames, decreased cylinder size, 20 psi higher boiler pressure, larger wheels and inside Walschaerts valve gear. The final number of locomotives in the class reached 175. Constructed by Crewe Works in May 1932, no. 49662 was allocated to Bolton shed from December 1957 until its withdrawal in May 1959. Bolton shed became an eight track facility in 1888 when four roads were added to the original structure built by the Yorkshire & Lancashire Railway. The shed closed to steam in 1968 and the site, located to the south of Bolton station, has since become a housing estate.

Preston 70052

Pictured before departure from Preston station is BR Standard Class 7 Pacific no. 70052 *Firth of Tay*. The locomotive was constructed in the final batch of engines (70045-70054) which appeared in 1954. In *British Railways Standard Steam Locomotives Volume 1* (2007), the cost given for these locomotives ranged between £23,446 and £23,987. This was an increase of nearly £3,000 over the first members of the class, which was due in part to a variation in the components used. *Firth of Tay* was attached to a BR1D tender, no. 986 when new, which cost £3,901 to build.

Left: **Preston 46250**
This view was taken from Fishergate Bridge, Preston, on 28 October 1962; it shows LMS Stanier Coronation Pacific no. 46250 *City of Lichfield* at the north end of the station. The city's first station was opened by the North Union Railway at the end of October 1838. It was replaced by a new structure in 1880 with an increased number of platforms and better facilities. No. 46250 was built by Crewe Works in May 1944. At the time of the photograph, the locomotive was allocated to Carlisle Upperby shed and had been there since October 1958. Withdrawal from there came in September 1964.

Below: **Blackpool Central Station 45565**
Ready to leave Blackpool Central station with the 13.45 Blackpool to Bradford passenger service is LMS Jubilee no. 45565 *Victoria*. The station was built for the Preston & Wyre Joint Railway, opening on 6 April 1863. It was originally referred to as Blackpool station, but in 1872 it became known as Blackpool Hounds Hill, and in 1878 it changed to Blackpool Central. The station closed on 2 November 1964 and was demolished and the site redeveloped. *Victoria* was built by the NBLC's Hyde Park Works in August 1934. It was withdrawn in January 1967, and had a few more years of service left when the picture was taken.

Blackpool Central Shed 45051

LMS Stanier Black Five no. 45051 emerged from Vulcan Foundry in November 1934. At this time it was fitted with a type 3B vertical throatplate boiler, no. 8668, which had a top-feed dome cover and 14 element superheater. After being in service it was found that the low-degree superheat was causing excessive water and coal consumption; locomotives built subsequently carried a redesigned boiler with the number of superheater elements increased to 21. It was also deemed necessary to rebuild the earlier boilers with 24 elements and a dome regulator in front of the firebox. No. 45051 carried this latter type between March 1937 and November 1939. When the photograph was taken during October 1964, a 21 element boiler was in use.

Blackpool Central Shed 45593

Blackpool Central shed was opened by the Blackpool & Lytham Railway in 1863 as a four track brick-built facility. The Lancashire & Yorkshire Railway rebuilt the shed with eight roads in 1885, and it remained in this form until closed by BR in November 1964 when it was demolished. Photographed at the shed a month before closure is LMS Jubilee locomotive no. 45593 *Kolhapur*, erected by the NBLC's Queens Park Works in December 1934. It left service in October 1967 and survives in preservation.

Blackpool North Shed 42638

Outside Blackpool North shed is LMS Stanier 4P 2-6-4T locomotive no. 42638, entering traffic from Derby Works in October 1938. The total length of the locomotives in the class was 47 ft 2¾ in. The engine could hold 2,000 gallons of water and 3½ tons of coal. No. 42638 was allocated to Blackpool shed from at least Nationalisation, and was withdrawn from there in December 1962. Fourteen other members of the class had worked from the shed during this period.

Blackpool North Shed 52415

Blackpool North shed (also known as Talbot Road shed) was erected by the Preston & Wyre Joint Railway in 1886 and contained three tracks. It had been in operation for seventy-eight years when it was closed by BR and the structures were removed from the site. L&YR Class 27 0-6-0 locomotive no. 52415 was built by Horwich Works in September 1900. The Class 27 was designed by J. Aspinall; between 1889 and 1918, 484 examples were constructed at Horwich. No. 52415 spent the 1950s working from Blackpool shed and saw further service from Bolton shed before it was withdrawn in March 1961.

Morecambe 45573

Morecambe Promenade station opened in March 1907 replacing a temporary terminus opened the previous year and an earlier station opened by the MR in the late 1840s. It was initially known as Morecambe station and acquired 'Promenade' in July 1924, before reverting to the original incarnation on 6 May 1968. At Morecambe Promenade station's Platform 2 in July 1964 is LMS Stanier Jubilee no. 45573 *Newfoundland*. The locomotive emerged from NBLC's Hyde Park Works in September 1934 and its initial allocation was to Crewe North before moving to Carlisle Upperby in October 1934. *Newfoundland* was allocated to Leeds Holbeck from April 1946 and left service from the shed in September 1965. The station closed on 8 February 1994 and was moved to a new site.

Hest Bank Station 42319

Hest Bank station was opened in September 1846 by the Lancaster & Carlisle Railway and consisted of a station house and three platforms. The station was closed on 3 February 1969 and the platforms have been removed, but the station house remains extant. Passing the south end of Hest Bank station during September 1963, at the head of a Windermere to Liverpool passenger train, is LMS Fowler Class 4P of 2-6-4T no. 42319. The engine was assembled at Derby Works in April 1928 but the boiler was constructed at Crewe Works and classed as G8AS (modified). It was 4 ft 8 in. in diameter, 11 ft 4¾ in. between the tubeplates, and operated at 200 psi. The locomotive was withdrawn in October 1963.

Hest Bank Station 76096

A BR Standard Class 4 2-6-0 is pictured in action with an unidentified passenger service. Erected as part of Lot No. 109, Horwich Works was responsible for bringing this locomotive to life and it entered revenue earning service in September 1957. Below the bufferbeam a protector plate can be seen signifying that the locomotive was fitted with AWS apparatus. *British Railways Standard Steam Locomotives Volume Two* (2003) quotes the cost of fitting AWS to the class as £335 per engine. No. 76096 also has electrification warning stickers and the top lamp bracket has been relocated. This suggests the picture was taken in the mid-1960s, before July 1967 when the locomotive was unavailable for any more portraits.

Carnforth 72007

Ten of the BR Standard Class 6 Pacific Class were built between 1951 and 1952 in the mould of the Standard Class 7s, but the 'Clans' had a smaller boiler, firebox and cylinders. A further fifteen were planned, but in light of BR's plans for rapid dieselisation, the orders were cancelled. No. 72007 *Clan MacKintosh* was built by Crewe Works in March 1952 and is photographed standing outside Carnforth shed in July 1964. *Clan MacKintosh* was a long-term Carlisle Kingmoor resident and generally worked as far south as Manchester and north to Perth. The locomotive was withdrawn from Carlisle in December 1965 and its final destination was the scrapyard.

Oxenholme 49382

LNWR Class B Four Cylinder Compound 0-8-0 locomotive no. 49382 was built at Crewe Works in December 1901 as LNWR no. 1899. It was rebuilt to Class G1 in June 1922 and was then rebuilt again to Class G2A in November 1940. The locomotive was photographed at Oxenholme Lake District station, which was opened on 22 September 1846 by the Lancaster & Carlisle Railway. It was known as Kendal Junction until 1868, when it became Oxenholme, but the 'Lake District' portion was not added until 11 May 1987. No. 49382 left service in September 1962.

Carlisle Canal Shed 60093

LNER Gresley A3 Pacific locomotive no. 60093 *Coronach* was built at Doncaster Works in December 1928. The A3s were an improvement of the GNR/LNER A1 Class; among other changes they had a superior superheater, smaller cylinders and were left hand drive. Twenty-seven were constructed, while fifty-one of the fifty-two A1s were rebuilt to A3 specifications. *Coronach* was withdrawn in April 1962 after a twenty-one year long allocation to Carlisle Canal shed.

Carlisle Canal Shed 61858

LNER Gresley K3 Class 2-6-0 locomotive no. 61858 was built by Darlington Works in April 1925. The design was based on the Great Northern Railway Class H3 with two cylinders; the new locomotives entered service in 1920 and were classified H4 by the GNR. The class had 6 ft diameter boilers working at 180 psi, 32 element superheaters, 18½ in. by 26 in. cylinders and 5 ft 8 in. driving wheels. Ten were initially constructed for the GNR before fifty were ordered from Darlington after Grouping. This group of locomotives, which no. 61858 was a part of, had North Eastern Railway features such as the cab, chimney and buffer style. The locomotive's time in service ceased in April 1961.

Carlisle Canal Shed 60813

LNER Gresley 2-6-2 V2 Class locomotive no. 60813 is ready to start work after an inspection at Carlisle Canal shed on 11 May 1958. No. 60813 was built by Darlington Works in September 1937, numbered 4784, and allocated to Doncaster shed. After a general overhaul at the latter town's works in December 1946, the locomotive re-entered traffic with smoke deflectors fitted around the chimney as seen here. This feature made it unique among the V2 Class. At the time of this photograph, the locomotive was allocated to St Margaret's shed, and could be at Carlisle after heading a number of different trains, including express freight, meat or even a passenger service. No. 60813 was condemned while at Dundee shed in September 1966.

Carlisle Canal Shed 64888

LNER Gresley J39 Class 0-6-0 freight locomotive no. 64888 came out of Darlington Works in September 1935. The class was divided into three parts when built, according to the type of tender the engine carried. No. 64888 fell into class part two as it had 4,200 gallon 7 ton 10 cwt coal capacity group standard tender. This example has straight sides, but a variation in this class part existed where the tender had sides that protruded at the top. The duties for the locomotives stationed at Carlisle Canal included local freight and passenger work, ballast, and pilot duties. No. 64888 left service in October 1962.

Carlisle Canal Shed 60068

Ready to head the Carlisle to Edinburgh portion of 'The Waverley' passenger service is LNER Gresley A1 Pacific Class locomotive no. 60068 *Sir Visto*. The service began in 1927 as the Thames-Forth Express, departing from London St Pancras and destined for Edinburgh Waverley station. Up to five of the class were on hand at Carlisle Canal shed for the service, which ceased in 1968. Construction of no. 60068 was carried out by the NBLC's Hyde Park Works in September 1924, and it entered traffic as no. 2567. *Sir Visto* was the last of the A1s (at the time classified A10) to be rebuilt to A3 in December 1948; the process of rebuilding had started in 1927, but did not gain momentum until the late 1930s. *Sir Visto* had left service from the shed after a twenty-two year allocation in August 1962.

Carlisle Canal Shed 65312

The Newcastle & Carlisle Railway opened the first shed in the canal area in 1837 and it was a modest one track structure. The North British Railway built Carlisle Canal shed to the west of Canal Junction and on the south side of the River Eden in 1862. The building was a roundhouse made of stone, measuring 150 by 175 ft, with a coal stage and carriage and wagon workshop also installed on the site. In 1910, and later in 1933, two and three covered tracks were brought into use respectively to accommodate further locomotives. The shed stopped housing steam engines in June 1963, and the buildings were demolished in 1964; the site has since become an industrial estate. NBR Holmes Class C 0-6-0 (LNER Class J36) no. 65312 was built by Cowlairs Works in March 1899 and withdrawn in November 1962. It was broken up at Inverurie in March 1963.

Carlisle Canal Shed 60535

The mechanical coaling facility seen behind this Peppercorn A2 Class Pacific was installed at the shed by the LNER in the early 1930s. No. 60535 *Hornets Beauty* was built by Doncaster Works in May 1948, joining ten already in service and preceding four that subsequently entered traffic. The fifteen Peppercorn A2s were supposed to be members of Edward Thompson's A2 Class (later A2/3), but when Thompson retired as Chief Mechanical Engineer of the LNER, the locomotives still to be built were redesigned by his successor. Apart from the first locomotive, named after the designer of the class, the names given to the engines belonged to racehorses that had triumphed at major races between 1905 and 1947; the locomotive's namesake won the 1913 Portland Handicap run at Doncaster. *Hornets Beauty* was withdrawn in June 1965.

Carlisle Canal Shed 69155

Originally this 0-6-2T locomotive belonged to the NBR A Class designed by William Reid; the class was split into two classes by the LNER at Grouping – N14 and N15. No. 69155 was built by the NBLC's Queens Park Works in August 1912 and was in the latter group. The N15s were in turn split into two parts on account of two different types of brakes used. No. 69155 was classed N15/1 as it was fitted with steam brakes only, while N15/2s had Westinghouse brakes. No. 69155's last shed was Carlisle Canal, and it was condemned in September 1962. It is pictured a month later on 28 October 1962.

Carlisle Kingmoor Shed 60100

After the closure of Canal shed, the former patrons of that facility were sent to Kingmoor to be coaled and serviced between duties. Gresley A3 no. 60100 *Spearmint* has been captured on the turntable in September 1964; it has probably travelled from Scotland with a goods service as it was allocated to Edinburgh St Margaret's at this time. Kingmoor turntable was installed by the Caledonian Railway in 1903 and located at the south end of the shed close to Etterby Junction. *Spearmint* and two other A3s were all that remained of this great class at the time, and the locomotive would only last until June 1965 when it was sent to be cut-up. No. 60052 *Prince Palatine* was the last to fall in January 1966.

Carlisle Kingmoor Shed 70002

In August 1964, BR Britannia Pacific no. 70002 *Geoffrey Chaucer* was at the head of a down freight to Gunns Sidings, Coatbridge (near Glasgow), when it collided into the back of a parcels train. This caused the damage that has been documented here during September 1964. There were no fatalities and the locomotive was repaired and re-entered service to Kingmoor shed. No. 70002 was not withdrawn until January 1967, and was later scrapped by G. H. Campbell, Airdrie, who cut nine other Britannia Class engines.

Opposite below: Carlisle Kingmoor Shed 45521

After its construction at Derby Works in March 1933 with a parallel boiler, no. 45521 *Rhyl* was rebuilt with a Stanier type 2A taper boiler, a new cab, and a Stanier tender in October 1946. Seventeen other Patriot Class locomotives were also rebuilt in the late 1940s. When this picture was taken outside Kingmoor shed, *Rhyl* was allocated to 8F, Wigan Springs Bank shed. This was the locomotive's last allocation, lasting from September 1961 to September 1963.

Carlisle Kingmoor Shed 42440

This image of LMS Stanier 4P 2-6-4T locomotive no. 42440 captures it outside no. 5 road at Kingmoor shed. The locomotive was built by Derby Works in April 1936. At Nationalisation, it was allocated to Aston shed, and in early 1950 it had reached Stoke shed where it spent the majority of the decade. In March 1958 it was at Kingmoor, transferring from Northwich, but only briefly, as it left in June 1959 for Barrow in Furness. Wigan was the engine's last allocation after residencies at the other Carlisle sheds. No. 42440 was withdrawn in September 1963 and then scrapped.

Carlisle Kingmoor Shed 70054

Dornoch Firth has probably completed the Leeds to Carlisle portion of 'The Waverley' service, and is being serviced before starting a return journey to its base at Leeds Holbeck. The early BR emblem is present on the tender but this would be replaced with the later emblem in March 1960. By this date, the handrails on the smoke deflectors would also be removed and replaced with hand holes. Kingmoor would be 70054's last allocation, which had started in January 1966.

Carlisle Kingmoor Shed 42542

Another LMS Stanier 4P Class 2-6-4T locomotive has been pictured at Kingmoor. No. 42542 was built by Derby Works in December 1935, one of the eight initial locomotives built with domeless boilers and a low degree of superheating. The total heating surface of these locomotives stood at 1,168 sq. ft. The locomotives with the modified design of boiler had a total heating surface of 1,366 sq. ft. Some of the initial eight engines subsequently acquired domed boilers, but the locomotive is seen here with its original type. No. 42542 was at Kingmoor between March 1958 and March 1960, and was one of only three allocated there after Nationalisation. No. 42542 left service from Newton Heath shed in July 1965.

Carlisle Kingmoor Shed 44767

No. 44767 was a distinctive member of the numerous Black Five Class, as it was the only one fitted with Stephenson valve gear. Trials were carried out to determine if the motion had any advantages over the Walschaerts valve gear fitted to the other engines of the class. It was found that there was no improvement in the performance of no. 44767, and the same application to other locomotives was not considered. No. 44767 had a number of other uncommon features when built at Crewe Works in December 1947, including a double chimney and electric lighting. These features were also found to be of no improvement over the existing design, and consequently they were removed in 1953. No. 44767 was condemned in December 1967 while at Kingmoor.

Carlisle Kingmoor Shed 42744

LMS Hughes 'Crab' 2-6-0 no. 42744 has been captured on 6 April 1957, having its tender replenished with water. The tenders for the class were of Midland Railway pattern and had a water capacity of 3,500 gallons and 5 tons of coal. However, this example is not modified to have coal rails, as were the majority of the tenders used by the class. The locomotive emerged from Crewe Works in March 1927 and was withdrawn from Hurlford in December 1962; it was used for a time afterwards as a stationary boiler before being sent for scrap. Next to the locomotive are the shed's snowploughs, and behind is another 'Crab', no. 42907, which is fitted with a small nose snowplough.

Carlisle Kingmoor Shed 57653

Kingmoor was opened fully by the CR in 1877 at a cost of £18,293, and the site was known as Etterby shed. Construction had started in 1874 and timber was used for the shed building, which replaced a smaller timber shed at Carlisle station. The design of the Caledonian Railway 300 Class, LMS 3F, was prepared by William Pickersgill, and construction began in 1918 and ceased in 1920. There were forty-three examples manufactured during this period. No. 57653 emerged from St Rollox Works as a new locomotive in July 1919, and was withdrawn from Kingmoor in January 1961.

Carlisle Kingmoor Shed 45582

The LMS type one mechanical coal stage seen behind Jubilee no. 45582 *Central Provinces* was installed in the late 1930s, and replaced a coal stage that dated from around 1895. No. 45582 was the first of the class to be produced at the NBLC's Queens Park Works in November 1934 and fitted with a Stanier 4,000 gallon tender. In *The Jubilee 4-6-0's* (2006) it is stated that in NBLC records, the water capacity of the Stanier tenders built by the company had a slightly lower capacity of 3,976 gallons. The locomotive left service from Carnforth and was dismantled at Crewe Works.

Opposite below: Carlisle Kingmoor Shed 45729

LMS Jubilee 4-6-0 no. 45729 *Furious* is in the south yard at Carlisle Kingmoor shed on 6 April 1957. The task of building the engine was given to Crewe Works and it was ready to start its career in October 1936. From nos 5702 onwards, the majority of the new locomotives were built with an altered superheater arrangement with 24 elements used, plus 159 small tubes of 1¼ in. diameter. *Furious* was also one of three fitted with new-build Stanier 4,000 gallon tenders – a type it is still attached to in this photograph. No. 45729 had been allocated to Kingmoor since 1937; it moved to Agecroft before it left service in October 1962.

Carlisle Kingmoor Shed 46244

In 1915, plans were prepared to reconstruct the timber shed in brick, using the original foundations. The cost of this undertaking came to approximately £23,000, and the task was given to P. and W. Anderson, who had completed the work by 1917. From then on, the name changed to Kingmoor shed. In Kingmoor's south yard, outside no. 1 road, on 28 October 1962, is LMS Coronation Pacific no. 46244 *King George VI*. It was allocated to Kingmoor from April 1961, and was in storage there between December 1963 and March 1964.

Carlisle Kingmoor Shed 42301

In the south yard on 28 October 1962 is LMS Fowler 2-6-4T no. 42301. The locomotive was the second member of the class to be constructed and was completed in December 1927 at Derby Works. The class had a problem with corrosion of the metal casing around the cylinders, and from 1940, the engines were fitted with cast-iron cylinder casing; no. 42301 received the new type in May 1945. The locomotive had been in service from Kingmoor since April 1961, and it was no longer required by BR a year after this image was taken.

Carlisle Kingmoor Shed 70012

Two Britannia Class Pacifics stand in the north yard at Kingmoor on 23 September 1967. No. 70012 *John of Gaunt* is devoid of its nameplate, which had been removed earlier in the year. Someone has taken pity on its classmate no. 70022 *Tornado*, and has applied the name to the smoke deflectors. The deflectors offer a contrast in the two hand-hole styles employed by the London Midland Region (no. 70012) and the Western Region (no. 70022). *John of Gaunt* and *Tornado* survived until the end of the year, when they were both sent for scrap.

Carlisle Kingmoor Shed 70014

This dramatic scene, captured again on 23 September 1967, sees Britannia no. 70014 *Iron Duke* coming off the turntable at Kingmoor. The 70 ft turntable replaced one of a smaller size that had only been in use at the shed for less than ten years. It had been installed at the expense of £620 in 1895, but it was recycled for further use at Guthrie near Aberdeen. No. 70014 was originally attached to a BRI type 4,250 gallon tender, however, in the intervening years it acquired a BRID type tender. *Iron Duke* is also seen with the original type smoke deflector handrails, and was one of a number not to be modified. Its nameplate is also missing and had been since mid-1964/early 1965, but it has been re-applied in paint. The locomotive was another casualty at the end of the year.

Carlisle Kingmoor Shed 92110

BR Standard Class 9F 2-10-0 no. 92110 was built in October 1956 at Crewe Works. The locomotive had a 6 ft 1 in. diameter boiler, a firebox of 7 ft 5½ in. long by 7 ft ¹/₈ in. wide, a superheater with 35 elements and 138 small tubes, two outside cylinders of 20 in. by 28 in. diameter, stoke with 11 in. piston valves, Walschaerts valve gear, and pressure set at 250 psi. No. 92110 went to work from Kingmoor during May 1965 and might have been found on fitted freight and parcels from Carlisle to Perth and Glasgow; mineral work, including limestone and soda ash, which was destined for Scotland. The engine was pictured on 23 September 1967 and withdrawal came in December of that year.

Carlisle 45212

Black Five no. 45212 is photographed with an 'up' freight from St Nicholas Bridge, Carlisle, during September 1967. Formerly on the site of the bridge was St Nicholas level crossing, where the LNWR lines, leading to passenger and goods stations, passed over the Newcastle and Carlisle Railway line. This was a busy and dangerous junction, and was the scene of a fatal collision in 1870, but it was not until the late 1870s that the crossing was eradicated. The locomotive was built by Armstrong Whitworth & Co. in November 1935, possessing a straight throatplate domeless boiler with a 21 element superheater. The engine subsequently carried a 24 element domed boiler three times during its career, and was fitted with one at this time, which it acquired in January 1966. Withdrawal came in August 1968.

Carlisle Bog Junction 44825

Black Five, no. 44825, was built by Derby Works in December 1944. It is pictured at Bog Junction, Carlisle, on the former Goods Traffic Committee Line from Willowholme Junction – the goods avoiding line built during a major re-planning of the city's railway lines in the late 1870s. From Rome Street Junction, the line was moved slightly to the south of the NER Canal Branch Line (formerly of the N&CR), so it could pass under a number of other lines. In the foreground is the Maryport & Carlisle Railway line from Forks Junction, while the passenger line of that railway goes over the bridge in the background. Bog Junction Signal box can be seen on the extreme right in front of the bridge. The lines past Rome Street were lifted in another reorganisation of the city's lines in the late 1960s. No. 44825 was withdrawn in October 1967.

Carlisle Citadel Station 45527

A Carlisle Kingmoor-allocated Fowler Patriot is illustrated at Platform 4 at the south end of Carlisle Citadel station during September 1964. No. 45527 *Southport* was erected by Derby Works in March 1933, and was withdrawn at the end of 1964. The locomotive was one of the rebuilt members of class and this occurred in September 1948 when it received a Stanier 2A boiler with pressure of 250 psi compared to 200 psi of the G9½S boiler originally fitted. The first station serving Carlisle was opened in July 1836 by the Newcastle & Carlisle Railway and was located close to London Road. The Maryport & Carlisle Railway and Lancaster & Carlisle Railway also used the terminus in the 1840s. It closed on 1 January 1863.

Carlisle Citadel Station 60093

LNER Gresley Class A3 4-6-2 locomotive no. 60093 *Coronach* has been modified by the addition of a double chimney, which was fitted in December 1958. The use of Kylchap double blastpipe and chimney was first tested on an A3 in 1937 when no. 2751 *Humorist* was fitted with the components. The chimney openings were 1 ft 5³/8 in. diameter, and the blastpipe was 5¼ in. diameter. It was not until May 1958 that orders were issued to fit the arrangement to the other A3s, and the modifications were completed by January 1960. A number of double chimney A3s experienced problems with smoke drifting, and were also fitted with smoke deflectors, but *Coronach* was among those not fitted with them. The locomotive had been involved in smoke deflecting experiments in 1931, with air entering the top of the smokebox and exiting behind the chimney, but this arrangement was not adopted on this or any other locomotive in the class.

Carlisle Citadel Station 42301

LMS Fowler 2-6-4T no. 42301, an Oxenholme shed resident, is at Carlisle Citadel station on 11 May 1959. During the development of the lines around Carlisle in the early 1840s, there were attempts by the Lancaster & Carlisle Railway to entice the other two companies present in the city to open a joint station. This would have also allowed the L&CR line to join with the Caledonian Railway, which was nearing completion of its line from Beattock, and would later reach Glasgow and Edinburgh. After many failed attempts with the other companies, the L&CR and Caledonian built a station adjacent to Court Square, which opened in September 1847.

Carlisle Citadel Station 10000 and 10001

Pictured inside Citadel station are nos 10000 and 10001, two prototype diesel locomotives built by the LMS and later classified D16/1 by BR. Both entered traffic from Derby Works in November 1947 and July 1948 respectively, and were designed by H. G. Ivatt. They had a CoCo wheel arrangement, a 1,600 hp English Electric 16SVT diesel engine with electric transmission, a top speed of 93 mph, and were 61 ft 2 in. long. The locomotives worked normal west coast services and for a time in the mid-1950s were tested against Southern Railway's diesel locomotives. Both were predominantly based in London; no. 10000 was withdrawn in December 1963 and no. 10001 left service in March 1966.

Carlisle Citadel Station 70018

When opened to traffic the station was not fully completed, and this did not occur until March 1850. When everything was taken into account, the cost stood at £178,324, with the CR contributing just under half of this. The other two companies eventually agreed to use the station and M&CR trains were admitted there in 1851. But the N&CR, by this time the NER, was not allowed access until January 1863. BR Standard Class 7 Pacific no. 70018 *Flying Dutchman* is pictured at Platform 4. It was built in June 1951 and is seen later in its career without its nameplate, with WR hand holes, and in an absolutely filthy condition. The locomotive was withdrawn from Kingmoor in December 1966.

Carlisle Upperby Shed 46237

No. 46237 *City of Bristol* entered traffic from Crewe in August 1939 streamlined, but this was taken off the engine in March 1947. It is pictured here at Carlisle Upperby shed on 28 October 1962, just before it started a period of four months in storage. The locomotive had only recently been allocated to the shed in April from Kingmoor, but had been to Upperby for a couple of spells previously. It spent a few weeks on loan from Camden shed, its main residence, in May 1952, before arriving for the second spell in June 1958. It was again stored between January and March 1964, and was sent for scrap in September.

Carlisle Upperby Shed 70025

Photographed at Carlisle Upperby shed on 28 October 1962 is BR Britannia Pacific no. 70025 *Western Star*. It was built by Crewe Works in September 1952, and the first allocation was to Rugby Test Plant where it underwent a series of trials. The locomotive travelled to Carlisle and Skipton for these, and some of the results are given in *British Railways Standard Steam Locomotives Volume 1* (2007). The steaming rate was 37,650 lb/hour compared to 30,000 lb/hour at the test plant. After 2,000 lb of coal was fired, boiler efficiency was 75 per cent, while after 3,000 lb this had fallen slightly to 72 per cent. Steam temperatures ranged between 720 and 737 degrees Fahrenheit. After leaving Rugby Test Plant, the locomotive was allocated to Cardiff Canton shed for the remainder of the 1950s. At the time of this visit to Upperby, *Western Star* was allocated to Aston shed. It was withdrawn in December 1967.

Carlisle Upperby Shed 46166

The LNWR shed at Upperby was in use for seventy-three years until it too was replaced by a new roundhouse installed by BR. The roundhouse had thirty-two tracks and at the centre was a 70 ft turntable. Closure to steam traffic came in December 1966 and it was demolished in the mid-1970s. Royal Scot no. 46166 *London Rifle Brigade* was erected at Derby Works in October 1930. It was rebuilt with a taper boiler in January 1945 and was fitted with BR smoke deflectors in May 1952. The engine was allocated to Upperby from May 1962, and is pictured there in storage with an empty boiler on 28 October 1962. No. 46166 was active until September 1964.

Carlisle Upperby Shed 46238

Pacific no. 46238 *City of Carlisle* poses for the camera on a line leading to the roundhouse shed at Upperby, in front of the shed foreman's office. The locomotive was completed at Crewe in September 1939 and streamlined; the engine and tender cost £10,838 to build. The 1X boiler barrel was 20 ft and 3¹/16 in. long, and tapered at the top and bottom from 6 ft 5½ in. at the rear to 5 ft 8⅝ in. at the front. When streamlined, the smokebox also tapered at the top in front of the chimney to allow the casing to be fitted. When the casing was removed from *City of Carlisle* in January 1947, the smokebox retained its taper for a few years before it reverted to the conventional style in October 1953. The locomotive was withdrawn from Upperby in September 1964.

Carlisle Upperby Shed 45279

Taken, probably precariously, from the top of a tender in Upperby shed yard, this picture shows LMS Black Five no. 45279 during July 1964. It was constructed by Armstrong Whitworth & Co. in November 1936 with boiler no. 9399, which had a separate dome and top-feed arrangement and a sloping throatplate firebox. Originally the atomiser steam shut-off cock would have been situated higher up on the smokebox, so it is likely to be carrying a later boiler. The two washout plugs on the first ring of the boiler are also a later addition as they were fitted to earlier engines between 1946 and 1952, while they were fitted to new-builds from 1944. The locomotive has the later style top-feed, which has been modified from the earlier type, and is missing the 'top hat' fairing so the setscrews can be seen standing proud of the centre. The locomotive returned to service after this spell in storage and was not withdrawn until March 1968.

CHAPTER 5

Corkerhill Glasgow to Stirling Station

Corkerhill Shed 57432

The Caledonian Railway 294 Class or 'Jumbos' as they were nicknamed, were constructed between 1883 and 1897. From 1882 to 1890, they were built to the design of Dugald Drummond, CR Locomotive Superintendant. Modifications were made to the design by subsequent holders of this office – Hugh Smellie, John Lambie and J. F. McIntosh. This example was built as CR no. 333 in October 1897 at St Rollox Works, later becoming LMS no. 17432, among the final batch built to the McIntosh design. The engine is pictured at Corkerhill shed, Glasgow, on 7 April 1957. It was withdrawn from Polmadie in October 1961.

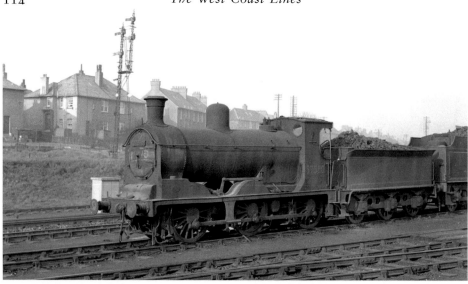

Corkerhill Shed 57580

This Caledonian Railway locomotive belongs to the company's 812 Class of 0-6-0s. It was built by Neilson & Co. in April 1900, following thirty other examples into service. A further forty-nine were constructed to the design of J. F. McIntosh at three other works – St Rollox, Sharp, Stewart & Co., and Dübs & Co. The locomotive was formerly numbered 842 before receiving no. 17580 from the LMS after Grouping. It had been in service for just over sixty-one-and-a-half years when withdrawal from Ayr came in November 1961.

Corkerhill Shed 40687

Corkerhill shed was on the southern approach to the station of the same name, and on the west side of the Paisley Canal Line from Glasgow Central. The line was opened on the former route of the Glasgow, Paisley & Johnstone Canal, which closed in 1881, and the line was opened by the Glasgow & South Western Railway in 1885. The shed was opened by the company eleven years later as a six track facility open at the ends and with a northlight roof. LMS Fowler 2P 4-4-0 no. 40687 was built at Crewe Works in October 1932 and was withdrawn in October 1961. It is pictured at Corkerhill on 7 April 1957.

Corkerhill Shed 40599

Photographed there in April 1957, no. 40599 was an established resident at Corkerhill. A number of Fowler 2P 4-4-0s were usually on hand at the shed for local passenger services until withdrawals began to claim them. Construction of the class had begun in 1928 with orders given to Derby Works, and in the three proceeding years ninety-eight were made, with Crewe Works also producing forty. No. 40599 was built at Derby in November 1928 and was in service until May 1959. Corkerhill shed welcomed steam locomotives until May 1967 when it turned its attention to diesels. The shed was demolished in the 1970s and replaced by a new structure for the stabling of electric locomotives and this has remained its current use.

Dawsholm Shed 57592

Located on the west side of Dawsholm shed on 7 April 1957 is CR 812 Class, LMS 3F, 0-6-0 locomotive no. 57592. Sharp, Stewart & Co. were responsible for building the locomotive and this task was completed in August 1900, when it was given CR no. 854. At Nationalisation, the locomotive was allocated to Carlisle Kingmoor shed, but it found itself at Dawsholm for the rest of the decade. Moves to Carstairs and Motherwell followed before its withdrawal in August 1963.

Dawsholm Shed 64520

Standing on the Repair Shop road at Dawsholm shed, next to War Department 2-8-0 no. 90436, is no. 64520, a North British Railway B Class 0-6-0. The class was a development of the Holmes-designed 0-6-0s and featured increased boiler and cylinder size. No. 64520 was built at Cowlairs for the NBR and was ready to enter service in November 1910. At Grouping, the locomotive passed to the LNER, who classified the locomotives J35. The class was subsequently superheated by the company and fitted with 22 element arrangements. Parkhead was the locomotive's last allocation and it was sent for scrap in September 1959.

Dawsholm Shed 57314

CR 'Jumbo' no. 57314 emerged from St Rollox Works in November 1889 and was in service until February 1962. It is pictured on 7 April 1957 next to no. 57592; behind the locomotive, the shed's sand store can be seen. On the right is the 50 ft turntable, which was installed when the shed was built in 1896 for the Caledonian Railway. The construction was carried out by R. McAlpine for the sum of £7,931, and the shed contained six roads with a two-road fitting shop on the west side equipped with a 40 ton lift. The shed closed on 3 October 1964 and the site is now occupied by residential properties.

Polmadie Shed 65221

During the 1870s, Dugald Drummond was Locomotive Superintendant of the NBR; he introduced a 0-6-0 that became the basis for this type of locomotive during the ensuing years. Matthew Holmes followed him into the role and modified the design slightly to produce the NBR C Class in 1888. These locomotives had an increased number of boiler tubes, amplifying the total heating surface over their Drummond counterparts from 1,061 to 1,235 sq. ft. This locomotive entered the class from Cowlairs Works in February 1891 as NBR no. 645. Construction of new locomotives to the design ceased in 1900 when there were 168 examples in traffic.

Polmadie Shed 70052

No. 70052 *Firth of Tay* has been photographed in Polmadie shed yard on 7 April 1957. From the shed, this locomotive and other class members allocated there would have worked between Glasgow and Perth and Glasgow and Carlisle. In January 1960, while hauling a train near Settle, the locomotive experienced a slide bar failure, which had been noted before as a problem for the class. As a result, the class and the Standard Class 6 Pacifics had their slide bar bolts strengthened and moved to make them more easily accessible.

Polmadie Shed 70051

Firth of Forth was allocated to Polmadie for almost eight years before it was moved to Corkerhill and then Crewe North shed. It is photographed here at Polmadie shed yard at the ash pits in April 1957; the engine would appear to be in preparation for its next duty along with no. 70052 and an unidentified Coronation Pacific (it carries a coat of arms or a crown above the nameplate narrowing the possibilities a little). There were four ash pits at Polmadie and they were 190 ft long. The ashes fell between grids on the pit floor into concrete hoppers, which then deposited them onto a conveyor belt submerged in water to cool the hot ash. It was then transferred by conveyor belt to a concrete silo 50 ft high and with a capacity of 50 tons, later to be deposited into empty wagons for removal. The ashpan on the locomotive could hold 50 cubic ft and was made up of three compartments.

Polmadie Shed 46203

The first two Stanier Princess Royal Pacifics were built in 1933; after they had been in service it was found that the small superheater fitted was far too inadequate for their operational requirements. From no. 46203 *Princess Margaret Rose*, built at Crewe Works in July 1935, onwards, the Princess Royals were fitted with a much larger superheater consisting of 32 elements. This gave a heating surface of 623 sq. ft compared to the 16 elements fitted to nos 6200 and 6201, which gave a heating surface of 370 sq. ft. No. 46203 was withdrawn from Carlisle Kingmoor in October 1962 and preserved by Sir Billy Butlin for static display at his Pwllheli holiday camp. In 1990 the locomotive was returned to working order and is currently owned by the Princess Royal Class Locomotive Trust.

Polmadie Shed 80114

BR Standard Class 4 2-6-4T locomotive no. 80114, built at Doncaster Works in December 1954, was the penultimate locomotive in a batch of ten erected there for service in the Scottish Region. Five were allocated to Polmadie, whereas the others were sent to Aberdeen Kittybrewster. From the former shed, the Class 4 2-6-4T could be expected to be scheduled on suburban passenger services around Glasgow, and to places slightly further afield such as Lanark, Edinburgh, Gourock, and Wemyss Bay. No. 80114 left Polmadie for Kittybrewster a month after this scene was captured in April 1957. It saw further moves to Keith, Hawick and St Margaret's before its withdrawal in December 1966.

Polmadie Shed 56039

Caledonian Railway 611 Class (LMS/BR 0F Classification) 0-4-0ST 'Pug' locomotive no. 56039 was the last of the type to be constructed for the CR in December 1908. The first had entered service in 1885 and was designed by Drummond (CR 264 Class); this example was produced by J. F. McIntosh. Forty were completed in total for shunting duties. No. 56039 was Yoker-allocated when the photograph was taken in April 1957; it left service in October 1962 from Dawsholm.

Polmadie Shed 56155

Located a mile or so to the west of Rutherglen station, Polmadie shed was erected in mid-1875 by the Caledonian Railway for the sum of £12,750. Timber was used for the structure covering the fourteen roads used to accommodate the engines. By the 1920s, the choice of timber had proved imprudent and a replacement was necessary. The new shed was completed in 1925 and was of similar proportions and capacity to the original, but bricks were used to make the building more durable. Further alterations included the refurbishment of the repair shops and provision of 35 ton cranes, as well as new water tanks and a mechanical coaling plant. The cost to the LMS came to roughly £112,000. This CR 498 Class 0-6-0T locomotive was built at St Rollox Works in March 1915 for use as a dock shunter. By September 1952 it had reached Polmadie, and was withdrawn from the shed in September 1958.

St Rollox Shed 57411

This image of no. 57411 was taken in April 1957 alongside the north wall of the locomotive shed, with a number of other 0-6-0s and a 4-4-0 on view. No. 57411 was built at St Rollox Works in October 1896 after the death of J. Lambie in 1895, when McIntosh made some modifications from the design of his predecessor's 0-6-0s. These included the reduction of tubes in the boiler from 238 to 218, and altering their size from 1⅝ in. to 1¾ in. Also, the motion, brake rods and chimneys were changed. The chimney on no. 57411 has been converted to a stovepipe type with the removal of the beading from the top; its original appearance would have resembled that of the 0-6-0 standing behind it. No. 57411 was removed from its duties in September 1961 while allocated to Oban.

St Rollox Shed 57240

Orders for the first six CR 294 Class were placed at St Rollox Works in March 1883. The first entered traffic in November and the cost of these locomotives, given by Cornwell (2011), was £2,000. This locomotive was part of that order and was completed in December with Ramsbottom safety valves housed in the dome and chimney with beading. The engine has subsequently been fitted with Ross pop safety valves and the chimney has been modified to the stovepipe type. Yet, it still retains its outside brake rods. The locomotive was released from service in October 1962 and cut-up at Inverurie Works.

St Rollox Shed 57251

No. 57251 (CR no. 354) has been modified to have inside brake rods – a change that was enforced by the LMS from 1935 – and has been fitted with steam sanding for the wheels. This latter feature was first introduced to the class by the CR, but later removed from the few engines that carried it. From 1926, the LMS began to make this alteration to the class, however, not all members were included and subsequently its use was curtailed because of problems caused by sand on the tracks and new signalling. No. 57251 also carries the smokebox door fastening clamps or 'dogs', which were again an LMS modification that followed on into the BR era. October 1962 was the month the locomotive ceased to be in service.

St Rollox Shed 73077

St Rollox shed, or Balornock as it is sometimes referred, was opened on 13 November 1916, eastwards of Buchanan Street station. The contract for construction was awarded to P. & W. Anderson, who completed the works for close to £28,000. The building had a slated multi-pitched roof and twelve tracks, with a repair shop adjoining the south end. A 70 ft turntable and coal stage was also installed on the site. At the shed on 7 April 1957 is BR Standard Class 5 4-6-0 no. 73077; it was a visitor to St Rollox from Eastfield shed. The locomotive was a 1955 arrival to Scotland; from Eastfield it would have worked the Glasgow Queen Street to Edinburgh service and the Highland service to Fort William. St Rollox received its stud of Standard Class 5s in the first half of 1957, and their main duty was the Glasgow Buchanan Street services to Aberdeen and Dundee. No. 73077 was withdrawn in December 1964 and St Rollox was closed in November 1966. The site has since been cleared of all trace of the shed, and the land has not been put to further use.

St Rollox Works 45100

LMS Stanier Black Five no. 45100 is at St Rollox Works in April 1957, minus its Mark 1 riveted tender. Construction of the locomotive was carried out by Vulcan Foundry in May 1935 and it was allocated to Farnley Junction then Newton Heath. The cab was 8 ft 6 in. wide and made from steel, with the roof's thickness $1/8$ of an inch. The driver's seat was made from oak and the gangway doors were originally fitted with rubber extensions at the bottom, but they were often removed and not re-fitted. The exterior of the cab has been fitted with a train staff holder below the open window. St Rollox Works was unique in that it applied 10 in. Gil Sans characters, whereas English works would apply ones measuring 8 in.; the positioning was also unique as it was in line with the running plate.

St Rollox Works 56025

Pictured outside its birthplace and place of employment is no. 56025, formerly CR no. 1515, a 264 Class 0-4-0ST. It was built in May 1890 and withdrawn in September 1939, only to be granted a reprieve and re-entered into service in November, when it became a St Rollox Works shunting locomotive. No. 56025 had 3 ft 8 in. diameter driving wheels, two cylinders of 14 in. by 20 in., and Stephenson valve gear. It weighed over 27 tons. The engine left service for the last time in May 1960 and was scrapped at Inverurie Works.

St Rollox Works 45175

A long-term Perth resident from the mid-1930s onwards, no. 45175 was a relatively recent addition to the engines available at Carstairs shed, arriving there from Corkerhill in February 1956. This image dates from April 1957 and locates the engine outside St Rollox Works. The works had been built in 1853 for the CR, but stopped building locomotives in 1927 when they became an LMS and then BR service and repair works. It has continued in this capacity to the present day. The locomotive was taken out of service in July 1963.

Cowlairs Works

A view of the interior of Cowlairs Works taken on 7 April 1957. To the left is the cab of no. 65908, a LNER Gresley J38 0-6-0 built at Darlington in February 1926. Behind is NBR Class G, LNER Class Y9, 0-4-0ST no. 68097 erected at Cowlairs in 1887, and withdrawn in October 1958. Thompson B1 4-6-0 no. 61402 is receiving attention to the rear of no. 68097. This B1 spent almost its entire career working from Dundee and went to Cowlairs for the majority of its works' visits. It is undergoing a heavy intermediate at this time; it arrived on 22 March and would leave on 20 April. A B1 is also present at the far end of the workshop. The works were brought into use for the construction of locomotives for the Edinburgh & Glasgow Railway, later building them for the North British Railway. Like St Rollox, after Grouping the works stopped producing locomotives and concentrated on repairing them for the LNER. It continued in this capacity for BR before it was wound down in the 1960s; work was finally transferred to St Rollox in 1968. Since demolition, the site has become an industrial estate.

Stirling Shed 56375

This dramatic scene has been captured close to Stirling shed and features CR McIntosh Class 782 0-6-0T no. 56375. The locomotive was built at St Rollox Works and was one of the final members of the class to be built. It was withdrawn from Stirling shed in August 1958. A Caledonian Railway shed had been present in Stirling since the mid-nineteenth century. This shed was made a through-road shed at the end of the 1800s with arched doorways, and in the 1950s it was partially rebuilt at the southern end. Stirling shed closed to steam in July 1966 and the site has since been re-utilised for commercial premises.

Opposite below: Stirling Shed 61998

LNER Gresley K4 2-6-0 no. 61998 *MacLeod of MacLeod* is photographed on Stirling shed's turntable in April 1957. The turntable was situated on the south-south-east boundary of the shed site and was 70 ft in diameter. It was an old fixture of Polmadie shed, replacing a 50 ft type at Stirling in the early 1950s. The K4 Class was first mooted in the mid-1920s for use on the West Highland line to reduce the amount of double-heading that was required to haul the increasingly heavy loads of the period. However, suitable motive power was found within the LNER's existing stock, and the idea was not advanced any further. In 1934-35, the idea was resurrected and earlier plans were utilised. The locomotives had 5 ft 2 in. diameter driving wheels to keep the axle load within the line's restrictions. There was a 5 ft 6 in. diameter boiler with a 24 element superheater and 18½ in. by 26 in. cylinders working at 200 psi to provide the necessary power. No. 61998 was built in January 1939 at Darlington, the final locomotive in the class of six. It left service in October 1961.

Stirling Shore Road Shed 62426

Belonging originally to the NBR Class J, the locomotive was one of twenty-seven built to the design of William Reid and equipped with superheaters. Sixteen had been built without them and were also part of Class J. At Grouping, the LNER divided the class into two parts – D30 and D29 respectively. The company also modified the superheater equipped engines to have 22 elements, reduced from 24. No. 62426 *Cuddie Headrigg* was made by Cowlairs Works in July 1914 and was one of the last of the class to be dismissed in June 1960. All Class J members took their names from Sir Walter Scott novels. Stirling Shore Road shed was closed in September 1957. It had been built in 1864 by the NBR and had remained little changed since that time.

Stirling Station 73120

Leaving the south end of Stirling station, BR Standard Class 5 4-6-0 no. 73120 is heading 'The Bon Accord' passenger service from Aberdeen to Glasgow Buchanan Street station. A product of Doncaster Works in January 1956, the locomotive spent the next seven years operating from Perth shed. It joined five already there, with two more joining them later. Typical destinations were Aberdeen, Glasgow and Dundee on passenger, post and fish services. The Standard Class 5s had left the shed by 1964 when they were displaced by diesels. No. 73120 was relocated to Corkerhill and was withdrawn from there in December 1966.

Bibliography

Baker, Allan C. *The Book of the Coronation Pacifics Mk2* (2010)

Bolger, Paul *BR Steam Motive Power Depots – Scottish Region* (2009)

Christiansen, R. *Rail Centres: Crewe* (2007)

Clay, John F. *The Stanier Black Fives* (1974)

Clough, David N. *British Rail Standard Diesels of the 1960s* (2009)

Cornwell, H. J. C. *The Caledonian Railway 'Jumbos': The 18in x 26in 0-6-0s* (2011)

Ellaway, K. J. *The Great British Railway Station: Euston* (1994)

Griffiths, Roger and Paul Smith *The Directory of British Engine Sheds and Principle Locomotive Servicing Points: 1* (1999)

Griffiths, Roger and Paul Smith *The Directory of British Engine Sheds and Principle Locomotive Servicing Points: 2* (2000)

Grindlay, Jim *British Railways Steam Locomotive Allocations 1948-1968: Part Three London Midland and Scottish Regions 40001-58937* (2008)

Haresnape, Brian *Fowler Locomotives: A Pictorial History* (1997)

Haresnape, Brian *Stanier Locomotives: A Pictorial History* (1974)

Hawkins, Chris and George Reeve *LMS Engine Sheds Volume Two: The Midland Railway* (1981)

Hawkins, Chris and George Reeve *LMS Engine Sheds Volume Five: The Caledonian Railway* (1987)

Hooper, J. *The WD Austerity 2-8-0: The BR Record* (2010)

Hunt, David, Bob Essery and Fred James *LMS Locomotive Profiles No. 3: The Parallel Boiler 2-6-4 Tank Engines* (2002)

Hunt, David, Fred James and Bob Essery with John Jennison and David Clarke *LMS Locomotive Profiles No. 5: The Mixed Traffic Class 5s – Nos. 5000-5224* (2003)

Hunt, David, Fred James and Bob Essery with John Jennison and David Clarke *LMS Locomotive Profiles No. 6: The Mixed Traffic Class 5s – Nos. 5225-5499 and 4658-4999* (2004)

Hunt, David, Fred James, John Jennison and Bob Essery *LMS Locomotive Profiles No. 7: The Mixed Traffic Class 5s – Caprotti Valve Gear Engines* (2006)

Hunt, David, John Jennison, Fred James and Bob Essery *LMS locomotive Profiles No. 8: The Class 8F 2-8-0s* (2005)

Hunt, David, Bob Essery and John Jennison *LMS Locomotive Profiles No. 14: The Standard Class Three Freight Tank Engines* (2010)

Larkin, Edgar *An Illustrated History of British Railways' Workshops* (2007)

Locomotives Illustrated No. 10: BR Standard Pacifics

Locomotives Illustrated No. 21: BR Standard Tank Locomotives

Locomotives Illustrated No. 103: The LMS 'Royal Scot' 4-6-0s (September/October 1995)

Quick, Michael *Railway Passenger Stations in Great Britain: A Chronology* (2009)

Radford, Brian *Rail Centres: Derby* (2007)

Radford, J. B. *Derby Works and Midland Locomotives* (1971)

RCTS *Locomotives of the LNER: Part 2A Tender Engines – Classes A1 to A10* (1978)

RCTS *Locomotives of the LNER: Part 2B Tender Engines – Classes B1 to B19* (1975)

RCTS *Locomotives of the LNER: Part 4 Tender Engines – Classes D25 to E7* (1968)

RCTS *Locomotives of the LNER: Part 5 Tender Engines – Classes J1 to J37* (1984)
RCTS *Locomotives of the LNER: Part 6A Tender Engines – Classes J38 to K5* (1982)
RCTS *Locomotives of the LNER: Part 6B Tender Engines – Classes O1 to P2* (1991)
RCTS *Locomotives of the LNER: Part 7 Tank Engines – Classes A5 to H2* (1991)
RCTS *British Railways Standard Steam Locomotives Volume 1: Background to Standardisation and the Pacific Classes* (1994)
RCTS *British Railways Standard Steam Locomotives Volume 2: The 4-6-0 and 2-6-0 Classes* (2003)
RCTS *British Railways Standard Steam Locomotives Volume 3: The Tank Engine Classes* (2007)
RCTS *British Railways Standard Steam Locomotives Volume 4: The 9F 2-10-0 Class* (2008)
Robinson, Peter W. *Rail Centres: Carlisle* (2004)
Sixsmith, Ian *The Book of the Ivatt 4MTs; LM Class 4 2-6-0s* (2012)
Sixsmith, Ian *The Book of the Royal Scots* (2008)
Summerson, Stephen *Midland Railway Locomotives Volume Four* (2005)
Townsin, Ray *The Jubilee 4-6-0's* (2006)
Walmsley, Tony *Shed by Shed Part One: London Midland* (2010)
Walmsley, Tony *Shed by Shed Part Four: Scottish* (2011)
Yeadon, W. B. *Yeadon's Register of LNER Locomotives Volume Six: Thompson B1 Class* (2001)
Young, John and David Tyreman *The Hughes and Stanier 2-6-0s* (2009)